WHAT NOW, LIEUTENANT?

LEADERSHIP FORGED FROM EVENTS IN VIETNAM, DESERT STORM AND BEYOND

BY GENERAL RICHARD 'BUTCH' NEAL, U.S. MARINE CORPS (RET)

PUBLISHED BY ADDUCENT UNDER ITS FORTIS NONFICTION IMPRINT

FORTIS

WWW.ADDUCENTCREATIVE.COM

TITLES DISTRIBUTED IN
North America
United Kingdom
Western Europe
South America
Australia
China
India

D0969662

WHAT NOW, LIEUTENANT?

LEADERSHIP FORGED FROM EVENTS IN VIETNAM, DESERT STORM AND BEYOND

BY GENERAL RICHARD 'BUTCH' NEAL, U.S. MARINE CORPS (RET)

FORTIS

AN ADDUCENT NONFICTION IMPRINT

WHAT NOW, LIEUTENANT?

LEADERSHIP FORGED FROM EVENTS IN VIETNAM, DESERT STORM AND BEYOND

GENERAL RICHARD 'BUTCH' NEAL, U.S. MARINE CORPS (RET)

ISBN 978-1-937592-63-9 (HARDBACK)

ISBN 978-1-937592-64-6 (PAPERBACK)

LIBRARY OF CONGRESS CONTROL NUMBER: 2016960813

PUBLISHED BY ADDUCENT UNDER ITS FORTIS NONFICTION IMPRINT

FORTIS 🏯

Jacksonville, Florida

www.AdducentCreative.com

Published in the United States of America

Cover photo: First Platoon Commander Lt. John Prickett and Lt. Richard Neal checking their position on their maps while on Operation Prairie III

TABLE OF CONTENTS

ACKNOWLEDGMENTS

DEDICATION

FOREWORD   i

PREFACE   1

CHAPTER 1
It Takes a Village   4

CHAPTER 2
From a Village to a Farm   7

CHAPTER 3
Back Home   15

CHAPTER 4
After My Father's Death   20

CHAPTER 5
College & Corps   23

CHAPTER 6
The Making of a Lieutenant   30

CHAPTER 7
VIETNAM | Going to War   34

CHAPTER 8
Operation Prairie III   41

CHAPTER 9
The Fight for Hill 70   46

CHAPTER 10
The Aftermath of the Battle of Getlin's Corner   57

CHAPTER 11
What Happened, Lieutenant?   62

CHAPTER 12
Coming Home   66

CHAPTER 13
Decision Time   75

CHAPTER 14
Back to Vietnam | Battalion Advisor   79

CHAPTER 15
Coming Home (Once More)   88
CHAPTER 16
Postwar Challenges   96
CHAPTER 17
A Marine Between Wars   102
CHAPTER 18
Wing Exchange Tour on Okinawa   110
CHAPTER 19
Amphibious Warfare School (Staff)   115
CHAPTER 20
Battalion Command   123
CHAPTER 21
Going Joint | U.S. Central Command   129
CHAPTER 22
Amphibious Warfare School (Director)   141
CHAPTER 23
When the Storm Broke   147
CHAPTER 24
Desert Shield: A Build-up for War   157
CHAPTER 25
Desert Storm   168
CHAPTER 26
After the Storm   187
CHAPTER 27
Back to Marine Headquarters   192
CHAPTER 28
2nd Marine Expeditionary Force   197
CHAPTER 29
Commanding General, 2nd Marine Division   204
CHAPTER 30
Joint Again | U.S. Central Command   214
CHAPTER 31
Assistant Commandant, U.S. Marine Corps   224
CHAPTER 32
Retirement: Moving On   242
AFTERWORD   248
ABOUT THE AUTHOR   253

ACKNOWLEDGMENTS

Writing this book has been a journey in and of itself, and it would not have happened but for the insistence of my children, Andrew, Amy, and Erin.

The life of a career Marine is a team effort. I could not have done it without my wife, Kathy. She put her career as a Registered Nurse on hold for almost ten years, was a single parent on many occasions while I was away, raised three children with love, care, and guidance that ensured they became college graduates and ultimately, wonderful parents in their own right. She battled Stage Three cancer without missing a beat, shepherded us through countless moves, and all the while served as a mentor and role model to countless Marine wives and families. As Kermit the Frog was wont to say, "It ain't easy being green," but Kathy and our three children sure made the journey rich, enjoyable and fulfilling.

I have to acknowledge the assistance of Vivien Cooper, who put me through countless telephone interviews and emails to pull my story out of me and Dennis Lowery, who introduced to me creative nonfiction and its ability to bring to life important people and events in my life.

There are also countless people from my life without whom this journey would never have begun. I owe a tremendous debt from my early years to the people of the town of Hull, followed closely by the men and women I had the honor to serve with and for in the United States Marine Corps.

DEDICATION

"From this day to the ending of the world,

We in it shall be remembered,

We few, we happy few, we band of brothers;

For he today that sheds his blood with me

Shall be my brother..."

~ William Shakespeare

THE VIETNAM VETERANS MEMORIAL - PANEL 17-E

"General 'Butch' Neal has given us a superb story. This great chronicle of his life and service to the nation's Corps of Marines has, in 2019, been selected to be on our Commandant of the Marine Corps Professional Reading List for all Marines, Lance Corporal through General. This story will greatly interest all warriors, young and old alike, and should significantly help our young leaders as they face the future."

—GENERAL ALFRED M. GRAY JR., USMC (RETIRED), 29TH COMMANDANT OF THE MARINE CORPS

"I read *What Now, Lieutenant?* early one afternoon and became so engrossed I turned the last page only a few hours later. Knowing of the author's remarkable and heroic career, I'll admit opening the book with some trepidation, because I've learned from experience that, unfortunately, a writer's grand intentions do not always translate to good writing. I'm happy to report that this compelling book is the wonderful exception. A page-turner for sure, it is candid and inspiring. The author's generosity, kindness, humility... his love imbues every page. Well done, Marine."

—WALTER ANDERSON, FORMER EDITOR OF PARADE

FOREWORD

In contemplating writing this book, the single thought that kept coming to my mind was, *what's the point?*

Over the years, many people have asked me to write about my experiences during Desert Shield and Desert Storm with General Schwarzkopf. My children told me on several occasions that they wanted a legacy book they could treasure for years to come and read to their children—my grandchildren. They gave me a book entitled *Legacy: A Step by Step Guide to Writing a Personal History,* with this note: "We've always thought you should write a book. You are a natural storyteller and have a gift for writing. Your life is so fascinating to us, and yet there is so much we don't know. We hope this book inspires you to sit down and do something you've always dreamed of doing."

So, I started to draft an outline of those people and happenings I thought might be of interest to my family. The things that had happened to me over the years in my journey from a small town in Massachusetts to the rank of four-star general and Assistant Commandant of the Marine Corps. As I worked on the project, it became clear to me that, in telling my story, there might be important lessons from my experiences and observations from my life of leading and leadership that could serve a broader audience than just my family. I had no interest in writing a book filled with golden rules or business management principles. Instead, I endeavored to highlight some of the universal lessons I'd learned, lived and taught throughout my life. That's when I answered my own question. The point of this book is to share my significant moments in hopes that it will be meaningful to my children and grandchildren as they journey through their lives, and meaningful to you on your own.

To my children and grandchildren, and you my reader, I say this: I hope by the time you read the last page and close this book, you will be left with the belief that there is nothing you can't accomplish if you stick with it and work hard. Nothing in life is easy, and there is no such thing as a free lunch. But, regardless of your starting point in life and the challenges or obstacles you may face along the way, everything can still work out in the end. There is nothing we can do to change certain unalterable facts of our lives, but one critical thing is always within our control—the ability to use the gifts and capabilities we do have in order to bring about the outcomes we desire. This saying, a Chinese proverb attributed to Confucius, is something I believe in as well: *"As the water shapes itself to the vessel that contains it, so a wise man adapts himself to circumstances."*

Preface

The Italian poet, and novelist, Cesare Pavese wrote "We do not remember days, we remember moments," and I agree. This book is a collection of moments—from events—that I assembled. After reviewing the manuscript, I was concerned it was more of a diary, and though it was accurate and readable, it did not adequately capture the impact or my reactions to a variety of *moments* encountered over a long span of time that defined who I am. While searching for a means to address my concern, I learned about the concept of creative nonfiction (a type of writing that uses literary styles and techniques to create factually accurate narratives). That's the solution I thought, and I believe I've accomplished my objective.

You may wonder about the title of what you're reading. It seemed to fit when I began writing, but I was surprised by how often my story, and my life, circled back to that singular *What Now, Lieutenant?* moment.

Wars, fought on a grand scale with global consequences, are made up of countless smaller battles and events. For the men who fought, bled and died in them they are not small—those little pieces of war—and the personal aftermath and their effect is beyond measure. I'm going to tell you a little bit about one such battle (covered in full detail later on). It pitted a North Vietnamese Army (NVA) battalion of 700+ men against the men of Company I, Third Battalion, Ninth Marines, Third Marine Division. Of the seven officers in the field at the beginning, only three walked out:

```
Something didn't feel right to me; I thought
it was more than a tentative effort by the
NVA just to harass us. "I think it's a prep
```

before they attack and that we should head back now before it's too late."

It was already too late. The number of mortar rounds increased and showered down on Hill 70. Interspersed with the sound of them impacting, we could hear the distinct sound of AK-47 rifle fire. A lot of it.

It was obvious this was not just some probing action as the volume of fire, and the sound of mortars grew. The gut thump sound of grenades exploding joined in and signaled that men were in close engagement. The command group was in serious trouble.

Captain Getlin was on the radio. "John I need you guys back here in a hurry and tell Butch to get us all the artillery support he can muster, danger close, on Hill 70." He hurriedly read off the coordinates.

"That's your location, captain!"

"Do it now! Danger close!" Getlin barked. "It's the enemy's position too, they're inside our perimeter! We'll try to get some separation and fall back to another defensive position."

We had already started back at full speed, retracing our steps over the same terrain we had just passed. As we moved on a run back to Hill 70, I had my radio operator beside me keeping pace as I called in a fire mission. We were nearly to command group's defensive position when we rounded a turn in the trail and ran right into a significant number of enemy troops, supported by a .30

caliber machine gun on wheels. They were
between us and the command group's position.

I was 24 years old, and this was my first significant combat experience (and surprisingly, what happened—what I was called upon to do, was something I never imagined. What came afterward defined me for the rest of my life). The fighting lasted six hours, and toward the end, we were almost out of ammunition. Those few hours changed forever the lives of the survivors, including me, and the next of kin of the men we lost.

That battle was the crucial event in my life; an ultimate *What Now, Lieutenant?* moment that taught me well and prepared me for challenges in the future. And I learned that they were not singular and found just in the military. They are representative of moments experienced at all ranks and positions both within the military and in the civilian world. Whether a lieutenant or general, college president or company CEO, *What Now, Lieutenant?* moments, though not as traumatic as mine, will happen and cause you to call upon your education, experience, training, common sense and judgment to respond appropriately.

That phrase... that question with all it entails and how one responds when it's asked of them... seemed to fit best as a title for what you're reading now. Seeing that question in the eyes of the men on Hill 70 that day is how I learned a most valuable lesson about leadership over the course of a bloody day in Vietnam, now more than 49 years ago.

Everything that happened to me after that day is now seen through that prism.

CHAPTER 1

IT TAKES A VILLAGE

"Home is where one starts from." --T.S. Eliot

I always liked that phrase—it takes a village—but was never quite sure what it meant until I prepared to write my story. In looking it up, I found it suggested that a child does not just grow up in a home raised by parents, but will also grow up with input and understanding from those who lived in their village. Regardless of their upbringing the child belongs to and is shaped by the community. That sounded like my hometown and the people that made a difference throughout my life.

Intuitively I knew that anyone going to read this story would not want to be burdened with endless pages telling about everything I did from birth until I actually joined the Marine Corps. That material, while interesting especially to me, might turn the reader off before they ever get into the heart of the book. However, I do believe that a little background on the environment and the people that influenced me along the way is both instructive and interesting, so I beg your indulgence and ask you to bear with me through these next few pages. I believe you will enjoy the detour.

The small town of Hull, Massachusetts sits on a peninsula that juts out into the middle of the Boston Harbor, placing it in strategic proximity to Boston and the water approaches to the city. The town is a forty-five-minute automobile ride from Boston or twenty minutes by water ferry. It was initially a seafaring town, but with the expansion of the railroad system and the introduction of the automobile, it became a resort town. Reached by rail, car or steamboat, Hull was a popular getaway for those who lived in Boston and wanted to escape to the beach for the summer. It had six miles of white sandy beaches and many coastal hotels; it even had an amusement park in the middle of town. The Kennedys had homes there, and so did Boston's famous mayor, James Michael Curley.

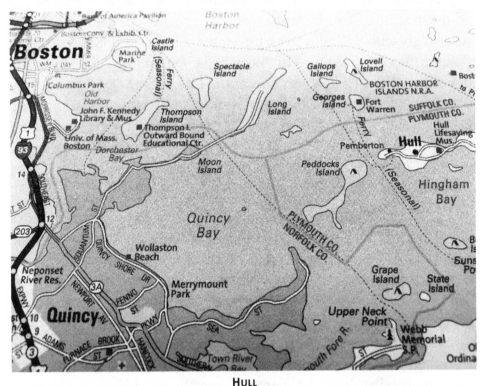

HULL

I grew up there during what could be characterized as a simpler time when a kid could just slam the front door and go outside to play with his friends. No one worried about the kids being outside after dark. During the winter months, there was a paucity of available friends, due to the small size of our peninsula town. There were only about five or six guys my age and we all lived in the Village which was on the extreme end of the town, if you went any further you would be swimming. My small circle of friends included Frank Yanizzi, his brother Johnny, Phil Thomas, Eddie Anderson, Eddie Hashey, and my cousin Bobby.

In thinking of them what stands out in my mind is the idea of loyalty, loyalty to each other. You could count on them to be there when you needed them and not surprisingly that remains true to this day. None of us ever got into serious trouble, and we all succeeded as adults in spite of the challenges each of us confronted along the way. After high school, Frank went into the Air Force and later became a police officer in town. Phil became a captain in the town fire department as well as a very successful lobsterman. Eddie Anderson went on to college and did very well in the business world as did Eddie Hashey in the seafood business. (His brother Artie would later marry my sister, Nancy.) And my cousin, Bobby, would serve in the Marine Corps and return to town and join the fire department. They were all I had, but what good friends then and now.

When summer rolled around, there was always an influx of kids from the city or surrounding communities. Our town's usual population of five thousand would swell to ten to twelve thousand as these families began to occupy their summer homes. Suddenly, we would have two or three times the usual number of playmates. It was like Christmas. Most of the kids that came in for the summer came from families that had boats and other recreational gear and playing with them was something we Townies really looked forward to. The most depressing day of the summer months was Labor Day because that was when everyone locked up their summer homes and went back to the city. Just as suddenly as the surplus of playmates had arrived, they would disappear, returning to their city homes and leaving me and my fellow Townies despondent until school was back in session.

Chapter 2

From a Village to a Farm

"How does it feel to be on your own, With no direction home, like a complete unknown, Like a rolling stone."

--Bob Dylan

1951

Hull, Massachusetts

When I was nine years old, I had a run in with my dad and what resulted led to my first *moment* of consequence in life. I believe the stress of his new job, meeting the mortgage payment on our new home coupled with the necessity of supporting a family of five, caused him to start drinking to excess. This had caused problems between him and my mother for several months.

One evening he came home, already 'feeling good' and wanted a drink, but mom had either hidden or smashed his liquor bottle. He became belligerent, which was completely out of character for him. Fearing that dad might strike her, even though he'd never done so, I physically inserted myself between the two of them. He was small in stature but compact and muscular, I guess wiry is the best way to describe him. I told him, "You'd better not touch mom!"

"You better disappear, young man," he said, "before I give you a boot or take a belt to your rear end!"

I was small in size too, but I wasn't about to back down. I told my dad, "No, I'm not leaving! You're going to leave!"

He looked at me for what seemed like an eternity, then pushed me away and left the house, probably in search of liquor. This event was in many respects long overdue. My dad had been drinking too much for some time, and just about every one of his friends did as well. They all were hard workers, grinding out a living usually with two or three jobs to support their family.

My mom and dad had bought this great house in Hull located on the water, and I believe the mortgage, in spite of the G.I. Bill, forced my dad to work even harder. To be fair to him, our family was a typical one for those days, Moms stayed at home and Dads worked. But the tension between my parents had reached an apex, and what had just happened between me and my dad forced a decision that disrupted what I was accustom to—my way of life—and everything drastically changed.

My mother was understandably upset over the friction between her and my father along with the conflict between him and me. The day after the incident with my father, she pulled me aside and said, "I talked to Aunt Harriett and Uncle Al, and I think it's best if we send you up to New Hampshire for a while."

Incredulous, I looked at her and said something to the effect of, "You can't be serious!"

She shook her head, not looking at me, and it wasn't at what I said. I think she was struggling with what she was trying to tell me. "Your dad has a lot on his mind. He needs some time to get... to get things under control." She stopped and looked at me for a moment. I had gone quiet with all the thoughts going through my head. She continued, "He feels terrible about last night and agrees with me that you going away for a while is best." She stopped again searching my face for what, I don't know. "You'll enjoy the farm, and your Uncle Al is a great guy." She said as she turned away from my room, "This will give us a chance to get the problems with your dad ironed out."

I could tell by the tone of her voice and look on her face that it was not an easy decision for my mom and dad, but to them it made sense. I had no doubts as to why I was going to the farm, but emotionally I couldn't comprehend why my parents would send me away. Making me leave my family and friends and go to a strange place where I knew no one but my aunt and uncle, and not even them very well.

I knew that my mom was doing this to keep peace in the family, not to punish me, but it was a hard thing to accept. I don't think dad would have made my life completely miserable if I had stayed at home but I believe my mother was concerned about the family dynamic going forward and feared an unhappy home situation for everyone.

Shortly after our talk I packed all my worldly goods in a small bag, and mom and dad drove me to the train station in Boston. As we waited for the train, my father seemed nervous—chagrined maybe— and paced the platform staying off to the side and away from my mother and me. He darted glances at me, and when our eyes met, I could tell he realized he was to blame for what was happening but couldn't tell me so.

All I could think about was that I was being forced to leave the world I knew. It didn't seem right or fair to me. My mother kept her composure and steadily reassured me that everything would be fine and that I would enjoy living with Aunt Harriet and Uncle Al.

They put me on the train and made sure the conductor knew I would be getting off at Concord, New Hampshire where I would be met by my aunt and uncle. I am not sure how long the train ride took because of the many stops along the way, but I do remember that I was scared and already homesick. I had never felt such a sense of loneliness as I did during that ride. It lingered for days.

NEW HAMPSHIRE

Disembarking from the train, I found Aunt Harriett and Uncle Al waiting for me. They knew the circumstances that had brought me to them and made me feel welcome from the start. There was a lot of small talk, mostly with my aunt as Uncle Al was by nature a quiet man, about everything but why I was there with them instead of with my parents.

I was going to have a great adventure while with them, is how my aunt put it. I felt deep in my stomach it was anything but that. We rode for about an hour and finally reached their house in the small town of Henniker whose welcoming sign boasted of being 'The Only Henniker on Earth!' I didn't know if it was the 'only Henniker' on Earth, but it sure seemed the loneliest and far, far from home. It didn't take me long to not just notice the differences. I could feel and smell them. Hull, my hometown, was a seacoast town where you could always sense and almost taste the tang of sea breeze as it came off the water and swept over you. And all my friends were nearby, close at hand, to share the adventures so important to the daily life of nine-year-old boys. From what I could see Aunt Harriet and Uncle Al's farm was in a rural area where there were few houses nearby, and thus no playmates or chance to make friends. Only cows and the smell of manure greeted me.

Their house was big with a huge adjoining barn and had been an inn at one time, so there were plenty of rooms for me to choose from. My aunt and uncle lived on one side of the house, and Uncle Al's parents lived on the other side. My uncle had served in the Army during World War II. When he returned to civilian life, he wanted nothing more than the simple life of a farmer, so he used the G.I. Bill to buy the farm from his dad, purchased a hundred head of Holstein cows and started a dairy farm. In the wintertime, Uncle Al supplemented his income by logging.

Uncle Al and Aunt Harriett weren't rich but the farm provided for their needs and they made a reasonable living. My aunt had three children from a previous marriage, all out of the house by the time I arrived, but Uncle Al did not have any children of his own. So, the introduction of a nine-year-old boy into his life was an awakening experience.

Right from the outset, he and I hit it off. He was about six feet tall, thin, wiry and strong; he had big 'farmer' hands and a boyish face that always seemed sunburned, summer or winter. I would look up at him as he talked to me and it was during those conversations that I learned much about farming and life. He had a special knack for explaining things to me without preaching or talking down to me. A good, and thoughtful, listener, blessed with amazing patience, he always had time to answer questions, explain things and show me what to do. At that point in my life, I badly needed a male figure and role model, and he was it. And, trying to gauge what the city boy was capable of, he did not place any limits or prohibitions on me.

He taught me everything about living and working on a dairy farm, from milking the cows to shoveling manure. He even let me keep one of the newborn calves to raise myself. That in itself was a lesson in responsibility. Not wasting any time, he showed me how to use the farm equipment. He would teach me what needed to be done and then it was up to me to do it or not. Even when I did something wrong, he never got mad over it or made me feel bad. Instead he took the opportunity to show me how to do things correctly the first time and more importantly how to do it better the next time.

Even though I was a young boy, he bought me a single-shot .22 caliber rifle and taught me how to shoot and use it safely while hunting in the woods. "Butch, the thing to remember about guns is that you must always assume they are loaded, so never in fun or through inattention point them in the direction of people, understand?"

My uncle even taught me how to drive a tractor and allowed me to use it to bale hay and plow the fields for planting. "I know that you are a bit young to be driving a tractor, but as long as you are on my property and you can reach the pedals to operate it, heck, I see no reason why you can't. Remember, a tractor is dangerous if it's operated foolishly, so don't ever be in a hurry to accomplish a task where going slow is safer, understand?"

That was how Uncle Al addressed everything, in a thoughtful and common sense manner. He shared his advice and experiences in such a way that it made me want to make sure I never disappointed him. After I'd been with them for a couple of days, he sat me down.

"Butch, I've been watching you, and I know you miss your family. Without any friends to play with I'm sure you're lonely, and that probably makes you even more homesick." He gave me what I soon came to recognize as his 'man-to-man' steady look. "I hope you and I become a team and that you can be my right-hand man in all that we do." He paused to make sure my eyes were on his. "I really need someone like you, to help me out."

That simple moment, being talked to that way and being asked to step up, struck a deep chord with me. "I'll do my best to help you, believe me." I nodded to Uncle Al.

Once I was settled in, instead of racing to play with friends as I had back home, I embraced with enthusiasm the chores I was now responsible for. Why? Simply because I enjoyed being around Uncle Al. His confidence in me was something I will always treasure. One day, in particular, stands out in memory. My uncle drove his tractor into a space between the barn and the fence with the intent of grading the space between the two. But, once he got it into that tight space, he couldn't get it out. He enlisted the aid of a neighbor who was also the town engineer and an experienced heavy equipment operator, but even he couldn't get the tractor out. Uncle Al said, "If anyone can get it out, I'll bet Butch can!" Sure enough, I maneuvered it out with very little effort. It was one of my greatest triumphs on the farm—and one of his, too. He was the one who had taught me to drive a tractor, and he was proud as a peacock when in front of the town engineer I was able to almost effortlessly drive it out. I was the son he never had, and it was obvious that he found great joy in teaching me all about farming and life in general.

My aunt was very different from him and didn't really fit what one would assume was the role of a farmer's wife. She was well-read, cosmopolitan in her outlook, and worked in a doctor's office in town. After I arrived she worked hard at helping me fit into my new environment. She helped me with my homework and we had great discussions on what she read. Along with my mother, she was responsible for my love of reading.

My time on the farm lasted about eighteen months. Right around that time, it came out in a series of telephone calls between mom and Aunt Harriet that both my mom and dad wanted me back home. Aunt Harriet came to me following one of those calls and said, "Well, it's probably time to get you back with your folks. I know they miss you, but you can bet that your uncle and I will miss you when you leave!" She tried to make returning home sound like a good idea much as she had to a very scared, much younger, boy just off the train from Boston some 18 months ago.

I had mixed emotions about returning home. I missed my parents and my sisters, but I liked farm life and had grown attached to my aunt and uncle. I was torn in two directions and obviously going home won out. With some reluctance, I prepared to return home to my family and school. But I was coming home a much different boy than had left it. My Uncle had infused in me a work ethic that has never gone away—it continues to 'stand me in good stead'—even nearly six and a half decades later. His unflappable can-do attitude and reserved nature along with sound judgment made a lasting impression on me and became a part of who I am. My Uncle Al engrained them in me through his actions and his deeds, and they became embedded in my approach to addressing any situation from that time on.

CHAPTER 3

BACK HOME

"Death ends a life, not a relationship." --Mitch Albom

1953

HULL, MASSACHUSETTS

During the year and a half, I'd spent on the farm, I had matured quite a bit. By the time I left, I was more self-assured and had greater clarity as to what I could and couldn't do. Thanks to my time on the farm and Uncle Al's confidence in me, my own had increased a thousand-fold.

I was ten years old and in the fifth grade when I returned home. Though still painfully aware of my size, I was always small compared to the other kids in my school, but never let that stand in the way of achieving anything I set my mind to. My time away had accomplished its intended purpose as things between my dad and me had become harmonious again. He had a lively personality, people liked him, and he always seemed to have a smile on his face. A good talker, I was always amazed how he could carry on a conversation. Everything was going well at school. I had always been a good student but, upon my return to school from the farm, my teachers noticed I was more dedicated than ever. The strong work ethic instilled in me by my uncle had carried over into my schoolwork. [In high school, I would be selected to be a member of the National Honors Society and was elected President of the Student Council.]

* * *

Upon my return, it was evident that the financial challenges were still there, but my dad met them by working even harder. He was very intelligent and once hired for a state highway position, he was able to

DAD STUDYING FOR YET ANOTHER PROMOTION EXAM

move quickly up the ladder eventually becoming the superintendent of a region of Massachusetts highways. I remember watching him study a lot prior to taking promotion exams. He would take me for rides in his state truck and often on weekends when he had to work for one reason or another, he would take me along. He had cut back on his drinking, and with the state job stability, his finances were under control. He was able to cut down on side jobs and begin to enjoy life. All in all, we were a typical lower middle class family.

Shortly after beginning my sophomore year in high school, my dad got sick. He was a heavy smoker, just about every picture we have of him he has a cigarette either in his mouth or in his hand, and he had developed a terrible cough. By the time the doctors took x-rays, dad's condition had progressed to the point where he needed to go right into surgery. Sadly, it was unsuccessful, and dad's surgeon told mom his condition was terminal.

I will never forget my mom rushing into the house that day while I was washing up. She started crying, "Your dad's condition is so serious that there's nothing they can do!" I felt I should do or say something but could not think of a thing to comfort her. She was right; it was a quick decline. There was no real hospice care in those days, so dad spent his last days in my parents' bedroom with my mom taking care of him. Dad was real popular, and many people came to visit him while he was sick.

As for me, I would pop into his bedroom, and we'd exchange a few words, but I was still a kid, mostly interested in hanging out with my friends and trying to stay out of trouble. It never occurred to me all the things he and I should talk about and the things we should, or could, say to each other. Soon that opportunity would disappear. Thankfully, the incident that had led to me being sent away to the farm was water under the bridge and long forgotten by both my dad and me.

Five years had passed, but dad and I were both typical New Englanders in that we were disinclined toward displays of emotion. I suspect he felt it went without saying that he now recognized he could count on me. Our goodbyes were silent and held inside. Then one day, while mom was out shopping, he asked me to sit by his side on the bed. "I know your mom has told you I don't have long to live."

I nodded but couldn't face him and looked away.

"It won't be easy for your mom and sisters once I'm gone, but I feel comfortable knowing that you'll help them. Your time at the farm with your uncle accomplished what I didn't." I could hear his breathing as he paused then continued. "He made you into a responsible young man and a son any father would be proud of."

Then I looked at him—though young I had learned that important things need to be said eye to eye. "I'll do my best to help mom, you can count on it."

I remember how pale his face was as he nodded and said, "I know that and never forget, son... I love you." He settled back on the pillow and closed his eyes.

Within four months of his unsuccessful surgery, my father was gone. He was only 42, and I had just turned fifteen years old.

* * *

Shortly before my dad's passing, I had begun working, and I have been ever since. I had all types of jobs and usually two or three at a time; from cutting lawns, shoveling snow, digging clams, to selling Christmas trees. In Hull, people rarely went to school beyond high school, so blue collar work was the norm and white collar workers were the exception. The townspeople often cobbled together a living with some combination of jobs, often as town employees, working full-time for the police, fire or highway department while using their free time to earn extra income at side jobs as construction workers, clam diggers or lobstermen. Everyone worked more than one job. Even the fire chief had a painting business on the side. There is something about that persona, throughout the close-knit community, that became a part of me from a very young age. That way of looking at what life is, without shirking, and doing what needs to be done to get on with it.

Perhaps my most unusual job began during my senior year of high school when I found myself working on a turkey farm, slaughtering turkeys. I had seen an ad in the paper and went and introduced myself to the owner of the farm. He reminded me of Uncle Al and seemed a really nice guy. We talked for a bit, and he liked the fact that I had farm experience.

"Well, I'm not sure you're going to like this job, but if you've lived on a farm, I imagine you've seen just about everything," he said. "It is kind of an interesting job. On weekdays, you'll need to come here after school, and your only job will be killing turkeys. On the weekends, you'll have to come in extra early to help me capture the turkeys in the big pens they live in, put them in wooden cages, and then take them to the slaughterhouse where you'll do your thing. I have to warn you; these turkeys are heavy as can be and they aren't going to let you cage them without a fight!"

It turned out that he was right on both counts. When a turkey arrives at your dinner table weighing ten pounds, it probably starts out weighing about 20 to 25 pounds fully feathered. Those big birds did not make my job easy. When I was actually able to get a grip on them they bucked and twisted in a fury of clawed feet and spur that raked my hands and arms. The whole time I worked there, every day and every turkey was a battle. During my time on my Uncle Al's farm, I had seen pigs and chickens killed, and had been taught by my uncle how to gut and clean birds and other animals. I was accustomed to the sight of blood and got on with my work. I was probably motivated more by the paycheck and unfazed by the gruesome nature of the work.

I did that work for a year or so during my last year of high school and then Ernie Minelli, a contractor who had been a good friend of my dad's, had a job opening. He owned a construction company but also had the contract for collecting garbage and rubbish in the town of Hull. He hired me that summer after high school, and I worked for him all the way through college. It was a great job because the pay was good—the contrast to my former work was a welcome relief—I worked outside, and he allowed me to work during summers and vacations and any time I was off from school.

Dad's friendship with Ernie Minelli had to have been the motivating factor behind Ernie ensuring that I had the opportunity to work if I wanted. That friendship and the fact I was not afraid of hard work and was dependable ensured steady employment for the next five years.

CHAPTER 4

AFTER MY FATHER'S DEATH

"In three words, I can sum up everything I've learned about life: it goes on." --Robert Frost

1960

Shortly after I graduated from high school and started commuting to college, an old family friend, Roger Means, who lived across the street from my grandmother, asked mom if she would be willing to move in and help him with his wife who had become bedridden with serious arthritis. He was the Chief of the Hull Fire Department and did not feel comfortable leaving his wife unattended while he was at work.

Mom knew Marie and Roger well, so she sold the house, and we moved in with the chief and his wife. Because their house was across the street from my grandmother's house, I knew the Means family well. They had three older daughters: Judith and Sandra, who were away at school at the time, and Elizabeth who was a year my senior and still living at home.

When I found out that we were moving in with the fire chief and his wife, I was happy—and relieved. Hull was where I felt most comfortable and where my friends and jobs were. I was always looking for work that would allow me to supplement my mother's income. All she had was a small stipend from the state combined with my dad's social security check. I also needed to earn money to keep my automobile running so I could get to and from Northeastern University in Boston, my daily commute. Between school and work, my time in the house was mostly for sleeping.

There was a secondary benefit to this new arrangement. Roger Means had a real impact on me. He influenced the way I thought, what I believed in and what I considered important. He always seemed to be there at the right moment to give me a kick in the butt, as well as some friendly guidance and fatherly advice. He was a dyed-in-the-wool Democrat so, just to keep our discussions lively, I decided I was a Republican. He would talk to me about how he thought Roosevelt and Truman were America's saviors, and I would expound on the merits of Eisenhower.

We had some wonderful discussions together, but I didn't realize until later in life just how wise he was and what a bearing he'd had on my life. In the absence of my own father, Roger provided a role model for me just as Uncle Al had done during my time at the farm. In retrospect, I can't help but feel that God brought these men into my life. No one could ever truly fill the vacuum created by the early loss of my own father, but there is no question that these father figures provided me with support and guidance just when I needed it. I will always remember an occasion while in college when I came home late one night after drinking with friends. Roger must have been waiting for the sound of my car in the driveway and was by the door when I came in:

"Butch, I know this is none my business since I'm not your dad. But I've grown to love you like the son I never had; I feel I have to give you some advice," he said.

I didn't want to hear it. "I'm tired and need to get some rest." I started to move past him toward my bedroom.

"This will only take a minute," he held his hand up, palm out. "You're putting your whole future at risk by drinking and driving." He shook his head never taking his eyes off mine. "You've got it made. You're getting a college education, and on graduation, you'll be an officer in the Marine Corps!"

I was still put out at the unsolicited—though well-meaning—advice. "I know that... so what's the problem?"

"Both your mother and I are worried that if you continue like this... you'll end up losing your driver's license and more seriously, jeopardize your future." He shook his head again and continued, "If that happens you'll disappoint an awful lot of folks; your mom, your grandmother... and me." He lowered his hand and stood there looking at me. "Please think about what I've said." He turned to head to his bedroom.

That night I did think about what he had said.

[Interestingly, Sandy Means, one of Roger's older daughters, married a Marine. When I was stationed at Camp Lejeune, and later in Okinawa on an unaccompanied tour as a young major, I would reconnect with her, her husband Jim, and their family. I visited their home so often that their kids, Michael, Brian, and Erin, came to call me Uncle Butch. We have all remained close ever since.]

CHAPTER 5

COLLEGE & CORPS

"Do not go where the path may lead, go instead where there is no path and leave a trail." --Ralph Waldo Emerson

1960 – 1965

Northeastern is a cooperative education university in which it took five years to attain your degree. The only downside to attending a five-year school was that my high school classmates graduated in 1964, but I wouldn't graduate until 1965. My major was history and education and the first year was no different from a traditional college. Thereafter, depending on your major, the school would find you a job that complemented whatever you were studying to become. Each of my four remaining years was divided into semesters: during one I was a full-time student, and the next I was a full-time teacher-intern. I interned at Silver Lake Regional High School, starting out in the school administration office and then becoming a teacher's assistant, and ended up teaching several classes as an adjunct faculty member.

My first year of college was paid for by a scholarship Northeastern gave me and I paid for the last four years with a combination of my job on the rubbish truck and my college co-op job. Those allowed me to graduate college, debt free. Not only that, but my intern job allowed me to graduate with almost two years of on-the-job training and experience as a teacher. It was a great way to receive a college education.

JOINING THE MARINE CORPS

In 1962, when I was twenty years old and in my second year at Northeastern University, I joined the Platoon Leaders Class (PLC) program. When you enter the Marine Corps via PLC, you attend Marine training at Quantico during your sophomore or junior years in college. If not for the offhand remark of a close friend I had known from high school, Frank Infusino, my decision to sign up for the program might never have happened. I was already enrolled in the U.S. Army Reserve Officer Training Corps (ROTC) program at Northeastern. My family history is one of service. My grandfather was in the Navy and later became a captain of a commercial ship. My dad and his four brothers all served during World War II, and my hometown of Hull had an Army base right in our neighborhood. I think all of these considerations led me in that direction. One day, while talking with Frank, who was attending the University of Massachusetts, he said, "Hey, I just signed up for the Marine Corps PLC program!" He told me about the program, explained what it entailed and said that it was set up to be completed in either one ten-week increment or two six-week increments during the summer(s) while you were in college.

Being able to complete the program in two increments was attractive to me because I didn't see it interfering with my work schedule. Had I not been a commuter, working almost full-time while attending college, I have no doubt that I would have probably stayed in the Army ROTC and never entered the Marine Corps. However, I was having a difficult time balancing commuting, school, ROTC and my job, so ultimately, my decision to switch from the Army to the Marines was purely a practical one.

Had I chosen the ten-week PLC program, I could have accomplished it over one summer. That would have been an attractive option if I'd had the ability to take off the entire summer, but I did not. I still had to earn money to help mom and pay for college, and I could not risk losing my year-round job as a rubbish man.

I opted to fit in my first six-week increment in the summertime when the high school where I did my college coop-internship as a teacher would be closed. That way, I wouldn't jeopardize my standing with Northeastern. By doing one six-week increment at a time, I was able to stay within the bounds of my internship program and still had half my summertime to earn money.

PLC was the perfect environment for me; as a commuter, I never went away to college or got to enjoy frat houses or the camaraderie associated with living in a university setting. My time at PLC was a complete departure from what I had experienced heretofore. Perhaps the novelty of experiencing a new and unique setting factored in, but I enjoyed PLC even though the training was tough and demanding. Obviously, no one likes to be miserable and those first six weeks were wretched but, at the same time, it was somewhat how I envisioned living at college would be like. I was away from my hometown, living with 30 other guys who were also in college. They were from all over the country, with different backgrounds, experiences, and expectations. But there was a bond in that we all had a common desire to be a Marine. My typical Boston Irishman demeanor—brash with quick one-liners—allowed me to be easily accepted by the other guys.

The Corps is not interested in selecting just anyone to be a Marine officer; they want someone who can tolerate the rigors of combat while at the same time effectively leading and commanding his or her Marines. The first three to four weeks of the PLC program were dedicated to identifying those who had what it took and those who did not. This was a weeding out process where we all underwent training designed to push each of us to our limits. Specifically, it was geared to challenge our physical, mental and emotional strengths and weaknesses. It flushed out those candidates who didn't have what was required and left those deemed good material for commissioning as Marine lieutenants. Anyone in the program who realized the Marine Corps wasn't for them could simply *drop on request* (DOR), which entailed walking into the office of the particular lieutenant or captain running your unit, and saying, "This isn't what I signed up for or expected!" That was all there was to it. You would be on your way home within 48 hours.

The brutal nature of my first six-week stint was exacerbated by a medical condition which was relatively minor but painful and highly uncomfortable. I certainly could have used my condition as an excuse to drop from the program. The fact that I didn't drop out despite my extreme discomfort probably impressed the staff. I underwent minor surgery and was allowed the time I needed to recover. I can still recall being in the squad bay during my five days on bed rest, and watching the other guys getting up and moving out to face another grueling day of training. I felt guilty lying around in my rack and was sure they would drop me from the program.

One day while the rest of the platoon were out training, the platoon staff sergeant paid an unexpected visit to our squad hut. When I saw him coming, I jumped out of bed and saluted.

Seemingly oblivious to the fact that I was completely naked he made a comment about my surgery, "I hear they cut you a new rear end candidate, that so?"

"Sir, Yes, sir!"

"They tell me you are on No Duty for four days, that right?"

"Sir, Yes sir!"

"You thinking you might want to DOR like some of the other pussies have?"

"Sir, No sir!"

Trying not to grin—and failing—he bellowed, "Get back up on that rack, Neal!"

The attrition rate was pretty high, and a surprising number of would-be Marines dropped on request. Several times, I wondered to myself, *why do I need to do this?* But quitting was not an option I ever considered. It seemed as if I always had to go the extra mile for anything I wanted, and there was nothing they could dish out that would lead me to DOR. There was no way in the world I was going to return to my hometown with my tail between my legs, having failed. The fact that many bigger, faster, taller and probably tougher guys dropped out or were weeded out while I managed to stay the course gave me a great sense of accomplishment and made me feel good. I was going to finish the program, come hell or high water.

* * *

In June of 1965, As I drove by the rubbish truck, I had to grin. When the guys on the truck saw me, they gave me big waves and smiles. I beeped my horn in reply and waved back at them. After all, that truck, and my work as a rubbish man for almost six years, had enabled me to afford college. It paved the way for a decision that affected everything in my life from that day forward; to become an officer in the United States Marine Corps.

I had just graduated from college. The event had taken place in the Boston Garden, a huge venue, and in addition to my mother, two of my uncles and my grandmother were in attendance. I was my grandmother's favorite, and it was obvious. Over the years growing up, I always found time to sit with her and listen to her stories. She was one tough woman, having raised five boys as a single parent. But as tough as my grandmother was, in her eyes I could do no wrong. For the ceremony, I wore the crisp white uniform I would be commissioned in, and I stood out in a sea of almost two thousand classmates garbed in black robes. [Twenty-six years later I would receive an Honorary Doctoral Degree from Northeastern for my service in Desert Storm.]

Upon completion of the graduation ceremony, I received my diploma, and as my family looked on, a Marine officer asked me to raise my right hand and repeat after him my commissioning oath:

"I, Richard I. Neal, do solemnly swear that I will support and defend the Constitution of the United States against all enemies, foreign and domestic; that I will bear true faith and allegiance to the same; that I take this obligation freely, without any mental reservation or purpose of evasion; and that I will well and faithfully discharge the duties of the office on which I am about to enter, so help me God."

GRADUATION AND COMMISSIONING DAY -- IN MY SUMMER WHITE UNIFORM

With that oath, I made a four-year commitment to be a Marine officer. My mother, assisted by the officer, pinned onto my uniform the gold bars of a second lieutenant. I was the first one in my family to get a degree and, though many men in my family had served in the military, I was the first to become a commissioned officer. That was a proud day, and afterward, we all went back to my grandmother's house for a wonderful celebration.

All of that ran through my mind as I passed the men on the truck and then watched them until they were out of sight.

CHAPTER 6

THE MAKING OF A LIEUTENANT

"Leadership and learning are indispensable to each other."

--John F. Kennedy

JUNE 1965

THE BASIC SCHOOL (TBS)

By the time, I arrived at the Marine Corps Base at Quantico, Virginia, the U.S. military was already in the early stages of ramping up the deployment of combat forces to Vietnam. Now my journey as a Marine was about to really begin. The base was a beehive of activity, and on the drive, out to TBS, I observed significant troop training activity in the woods and fields astride the road. Troops moved in formation in every direction, and everything I saw and heard was infused with a sense of urgency. I could see the Marine Corps was at full throttle, no doubt readying for possible combat missions in Vietnam. Even to this naïve lieutenant, it was apparent the focus of the training was singular: preparation for fighting the Vietcong. There was no sugar-coating of the fact that most if not all were headed for combat after The Basic School.

While completing my two PLC summer sessions, I was an Officer Candidate, but this time, I was entering TBS as a Marine Officer. It was a six-month course designed to teach us the basics of effective leadership, including such skills as land navigation, small-unit tactics, logistics, marksmanship, patrolling and familiarity with all of the weapons found in a Marine platoon and company.

At TBS, unlike PLC, there were designated leaders assigned to billets; positions that ranged from team leaders responsible for leading three other officers, all the way up to commander of the entire company of 200 lieutenants. All were evaluated on how well they carried out their duties. We were no longer Officer Candidates; we were now Marine lieutenants, with all the responsibilities that entailed.

The express purpose and challenge of TBS was to develop each of us into Marine officers who could effectively train, lead and command Marines. The situations designed to do so might be tactical, or any kind of scenario our instructors could think up (there is no limit to the kinds of mischief young Marines can get themselves into) that would give them an opportunity to gauge how we, as future leaders of Marines, would react to particular events or crisis. Whether it was a combat maneuver, a legal issue, or a Marine's family problem they were committed to developing us into role models, mentors, and leaders of Marines. This then was the task of the TBS instructors—to prepare us to meet these challenging responsibilities.

Approaching the TBS complex, I was struck by its collegiate, almost campus-like appearance. I thought to myself, *so this is where I am going to spend the next six months of my life before I probably go off to war!* The thought was sobering, to say the least. All one had to do was read the newspapers or watch TV to know America was already engaged in combat in Vietnam, and the deployment of U.S. forces to the region was escalating. With the conflict in Vietnam ramping up, there was no mystery as to where we would be assigned upon completion of training. One way or another, it was inevitable.

Throughout the six-month TBS course, we were constantly thrust into situations designed to force us to put into practice the instruction we had received in the classroom, and to answer the age-old question, "What now, lieutenant?"

That simple three-word query was on the mind of every lieutenant arriving at TBS. It was a source of some trepidation. Ever since I first made my decision to enter the Marine Corps, I had been asking myself it in various forms. I wondered, *how will I do in a combat situation? Will I be able to respond the way I've been trained? I know I'm going to be afraid, but will I be able to overcome my fears and lead my Marines?*

* * *

Everyone at TBS underwent the same training regimen. However, after TBS, the infantry officers were either assigned directly to an operational unit in the states or to Vietnam, whereas most of the other occupational specialties required follow-on school before assignment to a Marine unit (now infantry officers attend the Infantry Officers Course after TBS).

DECEMBER 1965

I finished TBS and returned to my hometown for Christmas leave, before heading to Fort Sill, Oklahoma for artillery officer's course and training to become a Forward Observer (FO) with an infantry company. While there, I got reacquainted with a girl I had always had my eye on, Kathy McCann.

Kathy and I had the same birthday, June 20th, and at her mother's insistence, we always shared her birthday cake. She was one of eleven kids, and she and her family summered in my home town of Hull each year, arriving there right after school let out in South Boston and staying until Labor Day. I met her brothers during their first summer, and we became friends. But that soon became a secondary reason for hanging out with them. It didn't take long for me to begin thinking that Kathy was the perfect girl for me with her short hair, freckles and those irresistible, flashing eyes. The trouble was I never thought she even noticed me!

That holiday season she had just returned home by bus from Mexico where she was doing missionary work after graduating from nursing school. She told stories about riding a donkey throughout the Sierra Madre mountains doing everything from delivering babies, to treating gunshot wounds, to pulling teeth. She described how mail was so important, and they were fortunate to have a pilot drop their mail to them from his plane. She told me how much letters meant to her, given her remote living conditions, and asked me to write. Listening about the conditions she worked in while there convinced me she was special. I promised to write and asked her to write back. As we parted ways and she returned to Mexico, I already knew I was crazy about her but wasn't sure about her feelings for me.

CHAPTER 7

VIETNAM | GOING TO WAR

"The one clear lesson of war is that when all is said and done the outcome of battle depends on the excellence of training, the quality of leadership and the courage of soldiers." -- General Gordon Sullivan, U.S. Army (Ret)

JUNE 1966 – MARCH 1967

Though it had been months since I had seen Kathy, thoughts and visions of her and home were still on my mind as I stepped onto the plane. There were so many threads of feelings and emotions swirling it's hard to pinpoint exactly the dominant one. When you're young, it's easy to not fully grasp how far reaching some of our decisions and actions are... I had only a small sense of that at the time. I did know that I was leaving a country of established peace and relative calm— all I had ever known—and entering a country at war. The world I faced when I got off the plane in Vietnam was going to be far different from the one I had just left behind the sealed aircraft's door.

My flight included a brief stop, just a couple of days in Okinawa until I was scheduled for a flight further down range, which was another way of saying... Vietnam. It was raining like crazy outside the Quonset hut they had assigned me a rack in. The sound was like fingers drumming on an empty coffee can, and it leaked so badly, that I might just have well slept outside. I didn't know it then, but it was good preparation for what lay ahead.

That first night I lay there listening to a radio playing in the hut. The song was *I'm so lonesome I could cry* by B. J. Thomas, and I couldn't think of a more appropriate song. I felt the same way I had when I was nine years old and on the train to New Hampshire. It was exactly—well, maybe a bit stronger—the same uncertainty and trepidation; that stomach in knots anxiety, wondering what was ahead for me. Only this time it was combat, not Uncle Al and a farm waiting for me. As vast as that feeling of aching loneliness was, the question I kept chasing an answer to, knowing I'd never catch it, loomed far larger in my mind. In battle, would I measure up?

* * *

The C-130 I was on landed in Danang, the Republic of Vietnam. I stepped off it, carrying my gear, into a sweltering heat. It and the noise were smothering. The cacophony of jets taking off and landing; the rush of people, military, and locals, all moving with the same sense of urgency, seen in Okinawa and on bases back home. In the distance, I could hear artillery fire. At what or who I did not have a clue—just a steady boom and thump in the thick air, rich with the smell of fuel, hot metal, rubber, and plastic. The sounds and confusion of a very busy airfield alone would have been plenty. Added together it reinforced that I had truly stepped into the unknown. Adrenaline pumped through me, heightening all of my senses. I had finally made it. Under my boots was that almost mythical land, Vietnam, I had seen on the news and talked about in training and with friends and family.

I reported in and was taken to a temporary hardback hut designated for officers. There were a number of cots for those of us transiting through on our way to assigned units. That first night the din outside, whether from planes landing or taking off, the firing of any and all types of weapons and the constant chatter of people passing by, made sleep futile. Several hours into my tossing and turning I was startled from semi-sleep by another young lieutenant, rushing into the hut calling my name. Seeing that I was the lone occupant, he came directly to my cot and shouted over the never-ending noise.

"Lt. Neal, we have a recon unit in trouble and need you to join a Sparrow Hawk platoon that may be launched to support them. I know you don't have all of your field equipment, but I'll get you a pistol and flak-jacket. We've already got a radio operator for you."

I had to ask him because I didn't know, "What's a Sparrow Hawk?"

"It's a platoon on standby as a Quick Reaction Force. With what's going on they felt they needed an FO." He gave me a steady look. "And that's you."

He left me to get dressed and then the pucker factor kicked into high gear. Here I was just hours in-country about to be flown into a combat situation to assist in the extraction of a unit in trouble; GULP!

Minutes later, the lieutenant returned with the equipment I needed. He gave me a map of the area with coordinates of the recon unit's location, radio frequencies and call signs of both the recon unit and the battery that would be firing in support. With him was my radio operator, who for obvious reasons did not seem excited about this mission or the rookie lieutenant he had inherited. As we stood there, gathering gear and our fortitude, we got word the recon unit was able to break contact with the enemy. The need for the Sparrow Hawk was cancelled. The three of us breathed a huge sigh of relief!

The next day I was flown south of Danang to the An Hoa valley to join Fox Battery, 2nd Battalion, 12th Marines. Because of my additional training as a forward observer and artillery officer at Fort Sill, Oklahoma, by the time I got to Vietnam and joined up with Fox Battery, most of my contemporaries from The Basic School (TBS) had already been there for four or five months. Right off the bat, I didn't care for the battery routine since our primary responsibility was to respond to calls for fire support by infantry units and I really wanted to be out there with the Marines going after the enemy. It was from this unit that I was assigned as a forward observer to Lima Company, 3rd Battalion, 9th Marines. I knew I would probably only have four to six months with the infantry before I would have to finish the remainder of my thirteen-month tour back in the battery as the fire direction officer or maybe even the executive officer. That didn't matter at the moment. I was finally going to a rifle company.

Lima 3/9

Being with the battery had not given me the feeling of being in the fight but, with this assignment, I really felt like I was about to do what I was trained to do. I was ecstatic.

Lima 3/9's commander was Captain Charlie Pyle, a loud, boisterous, profane, and at times obnoxious New Yorker with curly red hair and a nasty looking mustache. He stood about six feet tall and left no doubt about who was in charge. I soon learned he was a student of history and a true military professional. A superb company commander, he was a true warrior who knew everything about warfighting and went to extraordinary lengths to lead, train and take care of his Marines. He knew how to conduct tactical employment of troops, set up ambushes, and most importantly, understood how the enemy fought in the very difficult terrain of Vietnam. These were all things I had been instructed on at TBS, only now it was for real in a combat environment. Captain Pyle and the other lieutenants, including me, always argued over where we were on the map versus on the ground. My extra training at Ft. Sill gave me the edge, but boy could he read terrain and identify the most likely places the enemy might be. After getting over his brusque and brash manner, I found him to be a great mentor and role model.

MISSION JUST COMPLETED WITH LIMA 3/9

I stayed with Lima 3/9 for approximately six months and then, in the normal course of things, I rotated back to Fox Battery slated to spend the rest of my time as the fire direction officer (FDO). I was not happy leaving, but I knew and understood the process.

One day a new platoon commander with India Company, John Prickett, came over to the battery to meet our battery XO, Jim Tooten. They were both graduates of the University of Georgia, and it was during this visit that I got to know John and became convinced I would relish the opportunity to work with him.

In early January of 1967, our battery, and the 3rd Battalion we supported, redeployed from Vietnam to Okinawa for 30 days with three purposes in mind: to familiarize us with the new M-16 rifle we would be issued later in Vietnam, to join newly arrived Marines, and to enjoy some rest and relaxation (R&R). It was during this time I was able to reestablish my relationships with the Marines I had come to know in India Company and to meet some of the new platoon commanders in addition to John Prickett, specifically, John Bobo, Dan Pultz, Ray Gaul and the new India 3/9 Commander, Captain Mike Getlin.

Right off, I knew this was a terrific group of officers and the camaraderie that had developed between these officers and me while on Okinawa led me to request to my battery commander that I be reassigned to India 3/9 as their FO if a position became available. In particular, my friendship with John Prickett was one of the motivating factors in my trying to join the company to which he was assigned. As fate or destiny would have it, an opening in India 3/9 did materialize about that time and my battery commander reluctantly agreed to my request.

Shortly thereafter, we embarked upon Navy shipping and redeployed back to Vietnam, this time locating at Camp Carroll in the Con Thien Province, in close proximity to the Demilitarized Zone (DMZ) between South Vietnam and North Vietnam. As we were about to find out first hand, intelligence reports were correct in their assessment that significant enemy units were operating in the area.

It was great being with India 3/9, and I looked forward to operating with them. In my previous six months with Lima company, I had started to feel like I'd been let off the hook a little bit. My sole responsibility, as artillery FO for the company, was to call in the artillery when requested and to look after my FO team of a couple of young Marines. I was not the one who was responsible for how 30 to 40 Marines in each platoon were trained, fed or disciplined, or how they would respond in a combat situation. That was the infantry platoon commander's challenge. Knowing I wasn't expected to do anything beyond artillery made me comfortable and confident, almost to the point of being complacent.

But things—the situation—were about to radically change for me and the men of India 3/9. Circumstances would soon require me to assume duties and responsibilities well beyond those expected of an artillery FO and to summon all of my TBS training and the lessons I had learned while operating with the platoon and company commanders with whom I had previously worked. It was no longer theory or idle questions and answers (or the contemplation of them) ... it would be life and death.

Chapter 8

Operation Prairie III

"Nothing is easy in war. Mistakes are always paid for in casualties and troops are quick to sense any blunder made by their commander."

--General Dwight D. Eisenhower, U.S. Army (Ret)

MARCH 30—31, 1967
QUANG TRI PROVINCE - NEAR THE DEMILITARIZED ZONE (DMZ)

Shortly after returning to Vietnam we were given a mission in Operation Prairie III. Our assignment was to move as a company during daylight, looking for enemy forces reported in recent intelligence reports, and then to deploy into three platoon-size ambush positions after dark. We had seen indications of enemy activity, including footprints and discarded materials. The freshness of these sightings confirmed the enemy was in the area.

We had loaded out with three days of supplies including food, and water when we left our base camp, Camp Carroll. By late afternoon on March 30th, we had been on the move for the better part of those three days and were low on everything. It was hot, bloody hot; fry an egg on your helmet hot. The heat was as deadly as the enemy. We moved through the heavy elephant grass and choking underbrush, draining our canteens as quickly as we filled them from small streams we came across.

TOP ROGERS, LT. PRICKETT AND ME PREPARING TO MOVE OUT ON OPERATION PRAIRIE III

The company commander, Captain Getlin, passed the word there would be no medevacs for heat casualties. He encouraged and threatened his officers and non-commissioned officers (NCOs) to make sure their Marines drank plenty and at every opportunity refilled their canteens, while at the same time urging them to conserve water if possible. It was not a contradiction, but just a simple hard truth. We were all dragging from the heat and lieutenants, squad and fire team leaders were challenged in keeping the men alert and motivated. Fortunately, most had been in-country for some time and were combat veterans used to moving in such demanding terrain under such brutal conditions.

Michael Getlin had recently been promoted to captain just before he took command of India Company in January 1967. Probably about 5 feet 8 inches in height, and a medium build, he evoked a sense of quiet competence. He wore glasses (an unusual sight in that environment), carried his own shotgun, and possessed a confidence that made him appear older than his 27 years. He was not happy with the order to break the company into three platoons at night. He was concerned with the fresh signs of enemy activity in the area and felt strongly that keeping the company together made the best tactical sense. Not hesitating to raise his concerns, he spoke with the battalion commander and staff, but they stood their ground and said no. He had no choice but to reluctantly obey orders.

That third day, as night approached, he called us together and had his 1:50,000 map out with grease marks indicating where each platoon was to locate. We all made the same notations on our maps. In looking around the group, I was struck by how tired everyone looked. Our clothes were filthy and sweat-soaked. Once clean shaven faces, now grim with fatigue, were covered with three days' growth of beard. But each and every one of us was attentive to the captain and what he was telling us.

"All of the signs we've seen in this area indicate we may be dealing with NVA forces and they're known to be well armed and well trained. I raised this with battalion, but they still insisted on having our company set up three separate ambush sites."

Lieutenant Prickett spoke up, "Since battalion is so set on splitting us up and putting the whole company at risk, why don't we sandbag it and instead set up a company size ambush? Battalion will never know." John Prickett was the 1st platoon commander. Raised with three brothers in Toccoa, Georgia he was a tough, no-nonsense leader who radiated confidence. He was about my height, standing 5'6," with

JOHN BOBO AND JOHN PRICKETT

sandy hair and light complexion. He had a compact, rugged build and a command presence not often found in such a junior officer. His

43

mischievous grin was somewhere between a smile and a smirk and you never were quite sure which one was being displayed. A concerned leader who was well versed in platoon level tactics, he worked overtime to make sure his squad and fire team leaders knew their tactics and responsibilities, and their Marines were well trained. No detail was too minor in his eyes when it came to the men in his platoon. At the same time, he knew how to party and relax when the occasion presented itself, and while on Okinawa before returning to Vietnam, he and I had partied quite a bit.

Captain Getlin answered him: "To tell you the truth I thought about doing that. But I don't like disobeying orders. And more importantly, I don't like putting our troops at risk by not having them positioned where we're reporting them to be; it's too dangerous." He looked at each of us then back to John. "I want you to take your platoon and set an ambush site at these coordinates." He nodded at me. "I want Butch with you, since if anyone is going to run into trouble it'll be you. If that happens, you'll have a greater need for artillery support. I also want weapons platoon to augment you with a machine gun section, a rocket team and 60mm mortars."

He turned to the other platoon leaders. "Dan, I want you to send two squads from 2nd platoon to Top Rogers to reinforce the command group here on Hill 70 and for you and the remainder of your platoon to set up an ambush site north of our position at these coordinates." He looked at John Bobo. "I want your weapons platoon to augment Dan with a machine gun section, a rocket team and 60mm mortars." John Bobo was a quiet, reserved and soft spoken young man from Niagara Falls, New York. He was well-liked and respected by all who knew him. Mild-mannered, conscientious and sincere; to me, he epitomized the phrase Officer and Gentleman. Good-natured—despite the conditions—he had a down to earth approach to everything. Someone once described him as a truly good person, and I can think of no better description. I really thought he had missed his calling and should have been a priest.

Turning to 3rd Platoon Leader Ray Gaul, Captain Getlin said, "Ray, I want you to set up an ambush position east of our location at these coordinates; weapons platoon augment 3rd platoon also with a machine gun section, rocket team and 60mm mortars."

Captain Getlin looked up from the map, and his eyes swept over each of us, pausing just a second to meet our focus on him. "Ok, that's it, gents. I can't caution you enough about keeping your Marines on their toes." He rubbed his face then looked each of us in the eye again. "It's been a long day. If my instincts tell me anything, it's going to be an even longer night." He paused. "Any questions?" There weren't any and he took a last look at the map then began to refold it and put away. "Move as soon as you're ready, but I want you in your ambush positions no later than dusk."

CHAPTER 9

THE FIGHT FOR HILL 70

"A man does what he must in spite of personal consequences, in spite of obstacles and dangers and pressures, and that is the basis of all humanity."

--John F. Kennedy

MARCH 30—31, 1967

HILL 70

Nightfall was quickly approaching as I moved out with John Prickett's platoon in accordance with the plan. Just minutes later, we heard the unmistakable coughing sounds of mortar rounds leaving their tubes. We knew that they weren't ours. Since we were already some distance from the command group, we held our position and John made radio contact with Captain Getlin to ask him if we should return.

"Skipper, are you alright? Do you want us to head back your way?"

"No, it doesn't look serious at the moment," he said. "It's only a few mortar rounds; maybe a light probing by fire."

John wasn't convinced it would remain just a few rounds and started to alert the platoon to get ready to move out quickly in the direction we had just come from. He turned to me. "What do you think, Butch?"

Something didn't feel right to me; I thought it was more than a tentative effort by the NVA just to harass us. "I think it's a prep before they attack and that we should head back now before it's too late."

It was already too late. The number of mortar rounds increased and showered down on Hill 70. Interspersed with the sound of them impacting, we could hear the distinct sound of AK-47 rifle fire. A lot of it. It was obvious this was not just some probing action as the volume of fire, and the sound of mortars grew. The gut thump sound of grenades exploding joined in and signaled men in engagement. The command group was in serious trouble.

Captain Getlin was on the radio. "John, I need you guys back here in a hurry and tell Butch to get us all the artillery support he can muster, danger close, on Hill 70." He hurriedly read off the coordinates.

"That's your location, captain!"

"Do it, now! Danger close!" Getlin barked. "It's the enemy's position too, they're inside our perimeter! We'll try to get some separation and fall back to another defensive position."

We had already started back at full speed, retracing our steps over the same terrain we had just passed. As we moved on a run back to Hill 70, I had my radio operator beside me keeping pace as I called in a fire mission. We were nearly to command group's defensive position when we rounded a turn in the trail and ran right into a significant number of enemy troops, supported by a 30-caliber machine gun on wheels. They were between us and the command group's position.

The NVA machine gun opened fire—pouring rounds into our platoon—as we advanced. John Prickett was just ahead of me and was hit in the hip; they missed me and hit several Marines behind me. I called "Corpsman up!" as I knelt to help John. "Where are you hit?" There was so much blood it was hard to determine where it was coming from; I ripped off his shirt and saw the bullet hole near his hip. "Hang on John, Doc's on the way."

The enemy fire was intense as Lance Corporal Burghart, John's radio operator, and I tried to move him to a safer position. Almost immediately, while trying to stop the bleeding, Burgy was hit, and John was hit again. At the same time, an enemy soldier appeared seemingly out of nowhere. I reached for my pistol, but it was gone—it had come out as I had scrambled for cover initially or in my crawl to help John. I rolled over to an M-14 lying close by, thinking it was Burgy's. I brought it up and shot the soldier just as he was closing in on us with his AK-47.

Dropping the rifle, I crabbed back over to John and soon had blood all over me, as I tried to control his bleeding with my compression bandages and those from a couple Marines providing covering fire for us. He was in great pain, had lost a lot of blood and started to lose consciousness. I glanced and saw Burgy had already passed out. "Corpsman up!" I yelled again, but the noise from exploding grenades and AK-47 fire and the chaos of troops shouting and the enemy moving toward us made it difficult to hear anything. As twilight deepened the volume of small arms fire coupled with incoming grenades increased. Hell erupted around us. Mortar rounds rained down, and machine gun fire had pinned us in place. We were stuck. It was at this moment, as I continued to focus on saving John that I realized the Marines around me were looking expectantly in our direction—no, in *my* direction! They were very much aware their platoon commander was down, but they were ready to follow orders—my orders! That's when it struck me: *I was in charge whether I wanted to be or not!* With John seriously wounded, his platoon was now mine.

It had taken me a few seconds to fully grasp the position in which I found myself; these young Marines were looking to me for guidance, direction and orders. My *What Now, Lieutenant?* moment had arrived. Just then a corpsman scrambled to our position and quickly gave John a morphine shot and started to work on his wounds. Reluctantly, I moved away, and my eyes swept over the men closest to me. I had to lead.

"Rocket team up" were the first words out of my mouth. I realized we needed to silence the machine gun before we could counterattack since everyone was hunkered down due to the heavy weapon's fire. The call 'rocket team up!' went out man-by-man down the line. Before I could catch my breath, two Marines came scrambling, saw where I was pointing, and with rounds striking all around them, they fired and destroyed the machine gun with one shot. Once that was done, I felt we were in pretty good control of events. I started to maneuver the squads and fire teams as I had been instructed at TBS and as I had witnessed firsthand in previous firefights under Captain Pyle.

John Prickett had trained his squad leaders and fire team leaders well, and they quickly responded to my commands. They maneuvered their Marines quickly and professionally, counter-attacking and destroying the remaining enemy between the command group and us. This gave me time to call in artillery fire and coordinate air support. Up until that point, we had been unable to establish any further radio contact with Captain Getlin and feared the worst. First Sergeant Ray 'Top' Rogers was trying to get artillery support and air support on the same radio, and I told him "I got it Top, hold tight, we're coming to you!" Top Rogers was the senior enlisted alter-ego of Captain Getlin. He basically took care of looking after both the officer and enlisted Marines, from administrative issues to medical, to discipline. His genuine concern for each and every Marine was notable, and it's not overstating to say he knew every man in the company; their capabilities, strengths, and weaknesses. He was compassionate, yet a demanding, leader, and this was fully displayed during the battle on Hill 70.

UNCOMMON VALOR A COMMON VIRTUE

It is important to note that the Battle of Getlin's Corner was really two battles: the ferocious and heroic fight taking place on and around Hill 70 and the tenacious and relentless actions by first platoon, third platoon and remnants of second platoon to come to their rescue. The fighting these Marines experienced in their attempts to assist their fellow Marines was just as intense as that experienced on Hill 70. The *ethos* of taking care of each other that all Marines embrace was in full evidence during our counterattack toward Hill 70. There was no hesitation by these Marines in carrying the fight to the enemy in order to save their Brothers.

After knocking out the machine gun in our path, my Marines quickly gained fire superiority and took the fight to the enemy, swiftly eliminating those that stood in the way of our getting to Hill 70. We linked-up with the Marines from Dan's second platoon, and I instructed Dan to provide covering fire while we maneuvered across the open paddies between us and Hill 70 and to provide rear security for our wounded.

My Marines from first platoon closed on Hill 70, killing numerous enemy enroute. The air support was doing a great job of attacking the fleeing enemy, and this allowed us to move rapidly to where the command group was located.

When we found Captain Getlin, my worst fears were confirmed. He had fallen where he had established a position which best allowed him to control the fight, protect his Marines and deliver devastating fire on the enemy. He had died defending his Marines but not before he and his shotgun had made the enemy pay a heavy price. For his heroic actions, he was awarded (posthumously) the Navy Cross.

Likewise, when we found our weapons platoon commander, John Bobo. He was propped up against a tree with the bottom portion of his leg blown off. As we found out later, rather than allowing his Marines to move him back to a safer position, he had the corpsman apply a tourniquet on the remaining portion of his leg and then immediately stuck the stump of his leg in a hole he had scooped out in the ground to curtail the bleeding. From this exposed position, he provided covering fire so that his Marines could make it back to safety. By refusing to be moved to a safer position and staying in the fight, he was able to keep the enemy at bay while his Marines moved to alternate positions. His actions cost him his life but served as an inspiration to the Marines around him, as they carried the counterattack to the enemy. For this heroic act, he was awarded (posthumously) the Medal of Honor.

We also lost Captain Ralph B. Pappas, the forward air controller. He had joined us in Okinawa, and he and his team were true professionals. Unfortunately, he was an early casualty, killed just as he was calling in air support. His team was actually captured by the enemy but, with the help of gunships flying in support of us, we were able to drive the enemy off and rescue them.

Corporal John 'Jack' L. Loweranitis was part of the command group on Hill 70 when the enemy attack began. Tall, thin and gangly, he wore military issued glasses that looked coke bottle thick and were not designed for fashion, that's for sure. Out of the hills of Pennsylvania, he was fearless and rawhide tough and all who knew him respected and admired his fighting, rough and tumble persona. You could trust he would be there if you needed him; loyal and dedicated to the Marines around him, he was a fighting machine when the chips were down. He had already won the Silver Star medal for heroic action in September of 1966. This medal, along with the fact he seemed to always be getting into mischief when on liberty, made him a legend in the company. A no-nonsense kid, he was the type of Marine you wanted in storage to keep him out of trouble until war broke. He had been up and down the rank structure but was someone you wanted beside you if bullets were flying.

He proved this again on March 30–31st when Jack moved throughout the battlefield, first reorganizing the 60-mm mortar crew and delivering effective fire on the machine guns raking their positions, and then assisting with the evacuation of wounded while under intense enemy fire. Although wounded by small arms fire and grenade fragments, he moved to an exposed position to cover the withdrawal of the command group before being mortally wounded. Corporal Loweranitis went above and beyond the call of duty that day and was awarded (posthumously) the Navy Cross for his heroic efforts.

[In 2013, I had the honor of dedicating a barracks in the name of Corporal Loweranitis at the School of Infantry at Camp Lejeune, North Carolina. Recognition of Jack's heroic actions at this dedication ceremony was long overdue, and it is hoped the barracks carrying his name will serve as a reminder to the young Marines fresh out of boot camp of the absolute obligation and responsibility of every Marine to look out for his or her fellow Marines.]

Another member of India Company deserving of recognition was our Navy Hospital Corpsman Petty Officer Ken Braun, who was assigned to the company command group at the time. [The Navy provides corpsmen to the Marine Corps for support of all units; affectionately called Doc, they are invaluable in their efforts to treat and save the lives of Marines.] Doc Braun, at the age 18 was already a battle hardened, decorated combat corpsman before the Battle of Getlin's Corner. He was due to be transferred prior to the operation, but when asked by Captain Getlin to stay on, he readily agreed when told that the possibility of casualties was almost a given. Though seriously wounded at the outset of the attack, he still began administering medical aid to those around him. He moved throughout the bullet swept area time and again, treating the wounded and exposing himself to enemy fire. Totally disregarding his safety or his wounds, he refused to withdraw, fearlessly and skillfully continuing to treat the wounded while simultaneously engaging the enemy. With enemy troops all around him, he held his position and continued to assist a seriously wounded Marine until he was shot three times. For his actions, he was awarded the Navy Cross. [I was able to present the award to Ken Braun at a ceremony in 2005, at the Marine Memorial in Washington, D.C., a full 38 years after his heroic action. It seems the original paperwork for the award got lost, and it was only through the efforts of his Brothers from Getlin's Corner that the injustice was corrected.]

The final hero of many heroes during the battle was Top Rogers whom I mentioned previously. As the senior enlisted in the company, he normally stayed in the base camp to take care of the administrative requirements for the company and the Marines he served. He always wanted to go out with us and finally convinced Captain Getlin to allow him to be with us for this operation. We soon realized how fortunate we were, he was there. When Captain Getlin was killed, Top took over the Marines in the command group, got them organized to continue the fight, assisted in treating the wounded and established critical communications with battalion to request immediate air and artillery support. Though seriously wounded he nevertheless was instrumental in establishing a hasty defensive position from which he was able to recover many of his wounded Marines while at the same time coordinating critical air support. For his inspirational leadership, he would later be awarded the Navy Cross. [Jack Riley, then a corporal with the second platoon assigned to the command group and seriously wounded himself, was instrumental in ensuring these heroic acts were properly recognized and recorded after the battle.]

With the death of Captain Getlin, I now took command of India 3/9. Upon reflection, I might have thought I wasn't up to the task but my training at TBS and my time as an FO, for both Captain Pyle and Captain Getlin, had prepared me for just such an eventuality. I may not have been consciously aware of that training, but it was a resource I was able to call upon when needed.

This was the first time in my life I realized I was not invincible. Literally, overnight, I went from a cocky, carefree lieutenant to one who understood the power and responsibility of leadership and command. It was daunting. Any fears I had over being the one in charge were overcome by the urgency of the situation and, fortunately, I was able to do what I had been trained to do.

By this time, it was nightfall, and we no longer had the benefit of any light to assist us in our efforts to recover our wounded and dead. Of course, our greatest emphasis was on the injured. Knowing that there were Marines still out there, we formed three teams to go outside the defensive perimeter to hopefully find and retrieve them. There was no shortage of volunteers as everyone heard the cries for help from the darkness in front of our position. There was an almost unspoken knowing of what needed to be done, and they just went out and did it. They moved slowly and carefully through the darkness, even though it was clear we had beaten the enemy and those who had survived our counterattack were hastily retreating out of the area. In the meantime, I was still the FO and had ensured our artillery units maintained night defensive fire around our position and also kept firing at the fleeing enemy. I also covered the late Captain Pappas' duties, establishing contact with air elements and ensuring they provided air support.

Fortunately, the teams did locate several Marines that most likely would not have survived the night had they not been found and returned to our position.

Once we had an accurate sense of the number of wounded, I called for a medevac helo to pick up our most seriously injured. By then we were operating in complete darkness. With the assistance of Second Platoon leader Dan Pultz and several Marines, we cleared a landing zone. The problem was that we had to mark the LZ so the medevac helicopter could see it in the darkness. Fortunately, we had a supply of C-4, an explosive compound we used to blow up bunkers. Marines had learned that it could be safely ignited with a match or lit cigarette to produce a brilliant light but, more important, to heat their c-rations. We filled a couple of helmets with C-4 and positioned them on opposite sides of the LZ. When the chopper got close, we lit them and Dan assisted in guiding it in between the two burning helmets.

It was a CH-34, and I ran to it. "How many men can you carry?" I asked the pilot.

"Six or eight."

I directed Dan to get the fifteen men the Doc's had determined to be the most seriously wounded on the helo. It was so dark outside the pilot probably couldn't see how many men were being loaded inside and I didn't tell him. I wanted him to get all those men out of there. Once loaded, the helo lifted off slowly with me holding my breath until it had finally gained enough lift to clear the zone and was up and away.

Miraculously, all fifteen wounded Marines on the medevac would survive. Those whose wounds were severe but not life-threatening—over 30 Marines—remained behind and would receive immediate treatment from our corpsmen and would later be transported to base camp for more extensive treatment.

As I watched the medevac helo take to the air, I was relieved that my wounded Marines and sailors were on their way to first class medical treatment. At the same time, an oppressive sense of loneliness overcame me. My best friend, John Prickett, was on that helo and of the seven officers who were with India 3/9 when the battle began, only three remained. I looked at the men around me. There was still much to be done.

Chapter 10

The Aftermath of the Battle of Getlin's Corner

"The sorrow for the dead is the only sorrow from which we refuse to be divorced." --Washington Irving

March 31, 1967

Hill 70

Ray Gaul's 3rd platoon was still in close proximity to his original ambush site, so I instructed him to remain there until first light so as to avoid the possibility of being mistaken for enemy forces.

Dan Pultz and I located where the command group originally intended to set up and I had him handle the task of establishing defensive positions while awaiting daylight. At the same time, I was giving a situation report to battalion.

"Dan, I need you to insure our Marines are alert and in good defensive positions. I'm certain the enemy is gone, and we can go to a fifty-percent alert posture for the rest of the night. I've requested on call artillery fire, and battalion has assured me if we need air support, it'll be there. When you get back from making your rounds, I'll do the same, and you can monitor the radio traffic."

I was dead tired but did not sleep; adrenaline coursed through my veins. My mind was still trying to wrap around all that had happened in only a handful of hours. In them, suddenly, many of my friends had either been killed or wounded and flown out on the medevac helo. Overriding that serious thread of thought was that I now bore the full responsibility for every Marine on Hill 70. I wasn't concerned the enemy would return as I was confident we had inflicted heavy casualties on them and felt sure they had left the area under the heavy fire provided by our artillery and air support. My real concern was for the physical and emotional wellbeing of my Marines. Everyone had lost friends from officers, NCOs down to the most junior Pfc. What had occurred was not a PLC or TBS Leadership Reaction Course challenge, this had been real, and now I was the leader and commander.

* * *

When the sun came up, we scoured the battlefield to make sure we had recovered all of our dead and wounded. The final count that morning revealed that fifteen Marines had been killed and 47 wounded. We also had to retrieve all of our equipment that had been lost, discarded or damaged, do a site exploitation to retrieve any equipment, documents or other intelligence worthy items that belonged to the enemy, and attempt to determine the number of casualties they had suffered.

My immediate thoughts were focused on everything that needed to be accomplished before we moved out. But my mind continued to revisit the battle, recalling the chaos and heroics I had witnessed, while at the same time wondering whether I had correctly reacted, responded and led my Marines as demanded by the situation. Turning it over and over in my own head, I couldn't be sure.

In reflecting on the battle, I quickly realized in the span of 30 to 45 minutes I had gone from being a forward observer to being a corpsman treating John, to assuming command of his platoon and maneuvering it, to being a radio operator talking to battalion, to taking over command of the company while at the same time being the forward air controller. During those frantic and challenging minutes, fifteen Marines were killed, including two captains, one lieutenant, four corporals, two lance corporals, six privates first class and 47 Marines and Navy corpsmen were wounded.

I started to think through what needed to be done at the moment and accepted the fact I had to get the Marines moving. It was now my responsibility to get everyone reorganized and functioning. In order to do that, I had to get them more focused on the present than on their fear, confusion and grief over what had transpired. I understood the importance of walking around—being present in front of the men—and making sure the troops understood what had taken place over the past 24 hours.

I told Dan to gather the platoon sergeants and senior NCOs so I could talk to them. Once assembled, standing or kneeling in front of me were men who had seen death and destruction unimaginable in its extreme. They were dirty, some covered with blood—their own or that of their comrades—and the detritus of battle. Their hollow eyes were red-rimmed and sunken, as were their cheeks which were etched with only what I could assume were the tracks of tears. This motley group, the surviving leadership of the battle for Hill 70 stood mute before me, and I knew I had to be careful with how I spoke to them. They had just lost their company commander, two of their platoon commanders and many close comrades.

"I don't have to tell you that you and your Marines did all and more during this battle; you who were on and held Hill 70 and those who fought their way to assist and rescue the command group." My eyes stung, and I rubbed them before continuing. "We lost a lot of good Marines last night but the enemy paid a heavy price." I paused again, "Your Marines are tired and likely scared. For some of them, this had been their first taste of combat and of losing fellow Marines." I stopped because I felt it, too. I looked back up at them. "We all lost comrades. Never will it be more important than now that you help your Marines get through this. I need you to comfort while, at the same time, reminding them they are Marines; they must be ready to fight again if necessary." I let them know that, as difficult as it would be to stay focused and to continue the mission, I depended on them to make it happen. "I am so proud of you, and the Marines you and I are privileged to lead. Make sure you get my message down to them."

Some of the men that had knelt, now stood as I finished. "Battalion says transportation will be staged on the road nearby to move us back to Camp Carroll. Before we move out, make sure you have your Marines recheck the area for any equipment or ordinance. I don't want leave anything behind. We need to get everyone thinking, acting and performing as Marines which means cleaning their weapons and doing the things they have been trained to do." I looked at them arranged in front of me. "Any questions?" There were not any but the men, some of whom had seemed shaky minutes before, now seemed steadier. I nodded at them. "Let's get to it."

On that day, I became a great believer in eyeball-level leadership—facing people, looking them in the eye and listening to what they had to say. I had to keep in mind I was talking to human beings—tough young men—who had just gone through a life-changing experience, one that would be with them for the rest of their lives. Eyeball level leadership was an imperative that, from that moment on, became the dictum by which I lived during my entire career as a Marine Corps officer.

* * *

When we got back to base camp, it was depressing. Not only did we have to ensure all of the men were accounted for but we also had to inventory, clean and repair our weapons and equipment. The worst requirement was the necessity of gathering the personal effects of our comrades who had been killed or medevac'd. This felt like pouring salt on an open wound. It hurt like hell and brought back to center stage what we all had just gone through.

It was also at this time the full weight of what had occurred settled upon me. Not only was I trying to process the fact that of the seven lieutenants and captains in the field during the battle, only three of us walked out, I was also deeply troubled by, and unable to reconcile, the randomness of war. Why had some men lost their lives while some had merely been wounded or, like me, sustained no significant wounds except for some shrapnel in my fingers, which I removed myself.

It is said there are no atheists in foxholes, and I found that to be as true as it could be. Due to the horror we had experienced, there was no shortage of exhortations to a higher being. The Battle of Getlin's Corner did not rattle my faith, but it sure did test it.

It is difficult to articulate the sorrow brought about by the loss of all those friends. And that, in my case, it was complicated by having to make the sudden decisions involving the unit's complete reorganization necessitated by their loss. In the midst of all this, I was told to get cleaned up and to put on my best set of utilities (uniform). A helicopter was enroute to take me to meet with the division commander and his staff to discuss what had transpired on the night of March 30—31st. Given the number of casualties, Getlin's Corner was a significant battle, and there were a lot of folks that wanted to know in greater detail what had happened and why.

Chapter 11

What Happened, Lieutenant?

"If anything goes bad, I did it. If anything goes semi-good, then we did it. If anything goes real good, they did it."

--Coach Bear Bryant

April—May 1967

I went from the mud, mire and depressing environment of Camp Carroll to the relatively pristine conditions of the General's camp. There I was, a lieutenant, being questioned by a two-star general and his staff, trying to talk about something that it seemed, in many respects, they did not fully comprehend.

"Lieutenant Neal, I've read all of the Situation Reports on the battle but wanted to hear from you what you saw, heard and did during it. I understand that you were the forward observer and that the company commander had put you with the first platoon which was some distance from the command group. Is that correct?"

The nature and focus of the questions he and the staff were asking me seemed to be a veiled attempt to find someone to blame and hold accountable for our battle losses and injuries. This was going to be my second *What Now, Lieutenant?* moment as I went to great lengths to make sure that my company commander, Captain Getlin, didn't end up shouldering the blame.

"General, Captain Getlin had disagreed with the scheme of maneuver and, in particular, with the order to establish three platoon-size ambush sites. He'd raised his concerns with the battalion commander and his staff but was ordered to carry out his orders."

"As for positioning me with first platoon, he augmented all of the platoons with machine guns, rockets, and mortars. Because he thought first platoon might be the most vulnerable to attack, he made the decision to put me with them so I could call in fire support if it was needed."

"Why was he concerned with the orders to establish three platoon-size ambush sites?"

I explained in some detail what Captain Getlin had briefed us on before we moved out that night and specifically his concern over the evidence that NVA troops in significant numbers were in the area. I told him about the equipment, trash and fresh boot prints we had been finding in the immediate area.

"General, we knew they were there and in strength, and that was why our captain strenuously disagreed with battalion and why he assigned forces as he did."

That pronouncement seemed to satisfy the general and his staff, and there were no attempts to seek further information from me. I wasn't convinced that the general and his staff liked or accepted what I had to say, but I didn't have the energy at that point to try to weigh the outcome of the debriefing. The general wrapped it up and took me into the hut where he lived taking the opportunity to show me his washing machine! After getting me a cold soda, he said: "You know, Lieutenant Neal, from everything I've read you did an amazing job under terrible conditions and your Marine Corps is extremely proud of you."

I corrected him as tactfully as I could manage by saying that all of the Marines and sailors in India/3/9 did an amazing job during that battle and that the Marine Corps should be extremely proud of them; he quickly nodded in agreement. He was done with his one on one with me, and I left.

I later heard that there was a suspicion, at that time and at higher levels, that either the battalion commander or operations officer did not measure up to their responsibilities. Eventually, the battalion commander was relieved of command because the Marine Corps had lost confidence in him, no doubt as a result of what had transpired at Getlin's Corner.

* * *

It was during this visit to the commanding general's headquarters that I met Major Al Gray. In contrast to the general and his immediate staff, the major was quite interested in what had happened during the battle and, more importantly, what my thoughts were about what had occurred.

I didn't know him from Adam, and yet he sat me down and asked me about what went wrong, what went right, and what my actions were. Remarkably, he did not conduct himself as a typical staff officer but instead asked me penetrating questions about what had transpired on the night of March 30—31st. More importantly, he asked me what I would have done differently given the opportunity.

You can imagine my surprise. Here was a major asking me—a lowly lieutenant—what I would have done differently. He wasn't motivated by a "Who shot John?" mentality. He wanted to know what had happened so he could capitalize on and learn lessons from it. The major's questions were much more in line with what I'd expected the general to ask me. [Years later, Major Gray would rise to the rank of four-star general, become the Commandant of the Marine Corps, and end up pinning on my first star as a general.]

* * *

The next day, they held a formation for an awards ceremony and, to my great surprise, I was awarded the Silver Star. Typically, in the Marine Corps, it isn't until many months after an event that an individual would receive such an award, so the timing of this was quite unusual. Even as junior as I was at that time, I had the feeling that they were awarding me the Silver Star on that day as their way of saying, "Case closed, time to move on from this horrific battle."

In any case, I felt honored and couldn't help but feel that I received it for all the Marines of India 3/9 who had fought so heroically and gallantly that night. After the ceremony, I was flown back to Camp Carroll and rejoined India Company. After what we'd gone through on March 30—31st we were all a little antsy and nervous. There were a lot of new faces in the company, including a new company commander, a new first sergeant and several new platoon commanders, so it was difficult for me and many of the other Getlin's Corner veterans to fit in as comfortably as we had previously.

I had only two months left before I completed my thirteen-month tour. As you can imagine, they were the longest two months of my life. But they were filled with what was coming next in my life; my hopes and plans for the future. Kathy had returned home from her Mexico mission sometime after I left for Vietnam. Once I got to Vietnam, I was lonely as hell and started to write to her right away. When she started to get letters from me, she remembered how important mail was for her when she was in the remote region of Mexico, and she knew that I was experiencing the same loneliness. So, she decided to write to me once a week—just because it was the right thing to do. Her letters were a godsend, and I really looked forward to them. Although they dealt mostly with her job as a nurse and the activities of her family, I couldn't get enough of them. Her letters to me were not love letters, but when I wrote back, I started ending my letters with, *love.*

CHAPTER 12

COMING HOME

"A man travels the world over in search of what he needs and returns home to find it." --George Moore

JUNE 1967

As I walked up the moveable stairway and stepped into the 'Freedom Bird' (that is what we called the flights that took us home when we finished our tour) at the airbase in Danang, I had mixed emotions. Although I was happy to be leaving Vietnam, there was a sense of being alone. I would miss the men I served with, men I had come to love and admire. Unlike today's flights home (where, in most cases, you fly with members of your unit), here I didn't know a soul on the plane as the passenger list was determined by your overseas control date. Unless medically evacuated, you left Vietnam almost exactly thirteen months after you arrived.

At last, my date had come, and I was heading home. I could not be happier, but I was a much different man than who had stepped off that C-130, what seemed a lifetime ago. My happiness was tempered by a sense of guilt that I was leaving while so many remained. What really bothered me was that so much of my Marine Brother's blood remained in the soil of this far-off land. Again, the randomness of war plagued my thoughts. At that moment, I made a solemn vow that I would never forget those who had died on that fateful night and that if possible I would do all within my power to make sure that tragedies borne of leadership failures, such as we had experienced, would never happen again.

As I strapped myself into my seat, I thought back to that summer day in 1965, as I finished packing the trunk of my car with all my worldly possessions and said goodbye to my mom, my grandmother and my younger sister. Then I had hopped into the front seat and started driving through town on my way to Quantico, Virginia for six months of Marine Officer training. To say that I had mixed emotions about the trip, and the profession I was about to join would be an understatement. After all, I was leaving the comforts of home, leaving behind childhood friends, and leaving the town where I had lived all of my life.

While at TBS, I had made it known that the Military Operational Specialty (MOS) I wanted was 0302—Infantry Officer. In my mind, that's what being a Marine Officer was all about—leading Marines in combat! Even though I was very clear on the MOS I was interested in, each of us was required to make three choices for our MOS. Then, Headquarters Marine Corps would select our specialty for us based on three criteria: our performance at TBS, our Platoon Commander's recommendation, and most importantly, the needs of the Marine Corps. My three choices were infantry, artillery, and tanks, with the high expectation that I would get infantry. When the MOS list came out, I was listed for artillery. Words cannot adequately convey my great disappointment when I saw the list. I was so upset that I requested to see my platoon commander to plead my case to get this assignment changed. I can still remember going into Captain Pierpan's office. He looked up at me.

"I know why you're here, Lieutenant Neal. I'm as surprised as you are that you weren't selected for infantry." He was sympathetic. "I even recommended you for it." he shook his head. "I guess that your math background and the 'needs of the Marine Corps' are why you were assigned as an artillery officer."

"Is there anything you, or I, could do to change it, sir? Can I appeal?"

He had smiled and said, "I'm afraid not... but let me tell you something." He leaned back in his chair. "You'll get all the infantry experience you can handle as an FO, trust me. My FO in Vietnam was always at my side, and I relied on him as much as any other officer." He straightened and glanced at the paperwork on his desk then back up at me. "My advice is to just be the best FO there is. I'm positive it'll all work out."

The plane lifted off, and the thoughts of my MOS and Captain Pierpan's words faded as I fell into a deep sleep. I was headed back to 'The World.'

* * *

There were no family gatherings or welcoming ceremonies when I and others on my flight arrived in California, merely buses that would provide follow-on transportation to a commercial bus, train depot or airport for a flight to your home of record. I shifted myself and belongings from one metal tube to another for my flight to Boston.

Before reporting to Camp Lejeune, North Carolina my next duty station, I had 30 days of leave to do whatever I wanted. I first planned to meet my mother, my sister Pam, and Aunt Harriett and Uncle Al in Concord, New Hampshire. I must admit, I was in a hurry to get to Hull because I was sure that Kathy and her family were already there for the summer. Even though the many letters I had received from her could hardly be classified as love letters, they did give me cause for hope. So, after several days of visiting my family in Concord, I headed south to my hometown to see my grandmother, uncles, and many friends—and, of course, Kathy.

HULL MARINES: BOB NEAL, ME AND FRANK INFUSINO

HULL, MASSACHUSETTS

JULY 1967

BETTER YOU THAN AN INDIAN

I stayed at my grandmother's house while in Hull and as expected her welcome was just great; she was not bashful about showing her love for me. She confided to me that she and my uncles were planning a party for me that weekend and that they had invited all of my friends that had helped me along the way.

That afternoon, after answering all of my grandmother's questions and convincing her that I was in good health, I drove down to Kathy's parent's summer cottage. As I drove up, they were busy cleaning and preparing the place to move in for the season. It was great to see her brothers. Bill, Paul, and Frank had all been in the military, though none of them served in Vietnam. They, along with her brothers Joe and Mike, peppered me with questions about my thirteen-month adventure;

"Is Vietnam as hot as the news reports say it is? Are the people friendly to Americans?"

"What was the food like? Were you able to get anything you wanted?"

"Kathy told us that you were in a really bad battle. Were you wounded and were other Marines hurt?"

As much as I wanted to hang out with them and answer their questions, I could not help but blurt out, "So, where's Kathy?"

They said, "She just finished cleaning the house and left for the beach."

"Great, thanks. I was worried I'd missed her and want to thank her for being so good about writing me." I saw the grins forming on their faces. "I promise to answer all your questions later." I headed to the beach. All I had on my mind was she was so special that I thought for sure I could not measure up to other guys who had to be interested in her. I needed to find out about that as soon as possible.

When Kathy saw me walking toward her on the beach, she quickly jumped up from her blanket and plunged into the water. I immediately thought *Well, I guess that's that! There goes any romance I had in mind!* I came to the edge of the water. "Why'd you jump in?" At first, she didn't make eye contact with me.

"I was filthy from cleaning. I didn't want you to see me looking a mess." Her lovely face dripped water.

I nodded and after another moment's awkward pause she came out of the water and dried herself with a towel that had been folded on her blanket. She swept her hair back and faced me.

"Thanks for writing me." She was so lovely; I almost couldn't form the words. "You don't know how much your letters meant to me." An uncomfortable look came over her face, and my heart sank.

"I got nervous when you started signing them, Love Butch." She was twisting the towel in her hands. "But I'd promised you that I would write you."

My stomach was in knots. She was such a good person about it, in spite of my own spotty letter writing when she needed it most. I could tell she was uncomfortable, too, but there's only one way to deal with some things in life. And that's head on. "It's how I came to feel, Kathy. About you." I decided to keep going. "Are you free this evening?"

She met me my direct look without any sign of nervousness. "Yes."

So, with that inauspicious start, our relationship truly began. That evening we double-dated with her brother Joe and his future wife Anne—a schoolmate of Kathy's from nursing school and had a great time. During that month, Kathy and I continued to date, and it was obvious that we clicked.

That weekend my grandmother's party for me took place at the family home. She and my uncles had invited all of the folks in town who had at one time or another helped me along the way after the death of my dad. In addition to my mom, Aunt Harriet and Uncle Al, there was Roger Means, Ernie Minelli and a host of Townies who lived in the village and who I had known for years. These were the folks who had an impact on my life, and I could not have been happier in seeing them all once more.

MY MOTHER AND ME

The local newspaper editor of the town's weekly paper was

there to do a story on my time in Vietnam. Evidently the Marine Corps had sent out a public affairs news release to the paper on my award, so he wanted to do a story on it. I really didn't want to talk about the 30-31 March battle. That story was not one I was ready to share. Other than saying that a lot of good men did brave deeds that night I refrained from elaborating. Nevertheless, it was front page including the award write up. The best part of it was that there was a great picture of my mom and me cooking over the grill.

The 30 days of leave literally flew by, and I dreaded the thought of leaving Kathy. She was someone I wanted to spend the rest of my life with, but I was not sure she shared the same feelings. I had to find out. One evening, toward the end of my leave, while we were sitting on the seawall near her cottage, I asked her if she would marry me. To my great relief and joy, she said yes.

At first, I was shocked. It was the answer I had hoped for, but it stopped my thoughts for a moment. Then the next step was clear for me. "Well," I said, "I'd better go over and see your dad." [Kathy contends that when I proposed to her, I told her I'd get out of the Marine Corps in six months; I've denied ever saying that!]

Kathy's mom and dad were visiting at the home of Kathy's uncle, Paul, who had a cottage just down the street. From where Kathy and I were sitting on the seawall, we could see her Uncle Paul's house and when her folks left to head back to theirs. Once we saw them, we hustled over to catch them before they headed to bed.

I got up my nerve and said, "Mr. McCann, I would like your permission to marry Kathy."

He looked at me and said, "Well, better you than an Indian!"

That sounded like a 'yes' to me, but I didn't understand the significance of that statement until Kathy explained to me that her father had always worried that she'd find someone in the mountains of Mexico and marry him. Likewise, as she was growing up, he had always told her, "Stay away from those village guys. They don't even wear shoes!" Now, there I was, a village guy, asking for his daughter's hand in marriage. Nevertheless, both he and Kathy's mom were happy over news of the proposal and gave us their full support.

Kathy immediately got busy making the wedding arrangements, though I have to think that she had at least a few concerns about the prospect of marrying this 'crazy' Marine. We had decided we wanted to have the wedding in November, a short three months away. It all happened so quickly that when Kathy told her sisters, Helen who was a nun asked, "Who are you marrying?" When Kathy replied, her other sister Nancy responded, "I thought he was Joe's friend."

While Kathy was planning our wedding, I had my hands full fending off the urgings of my bachelor friends at Camp Lejeune, who wanted me to call off the wedding and continue to raise hell with them. And believe me, given the endless fun we were having at the time, that was no easy chore. They (and I) were making up for lost time—thirteen months in Vietnam—and trying to drown memories of things seen and done there. Though some of them were still recovering from serious wounds, we were all so happy to be alive. They all tried to convince me to stay single, but now that I had a 'Yes' from Kathy, there was no stopping.

I asked John Prickett to be the best man, and the sword bearers were all single guys that I hung out with at Camp Lejeune. I figured they would have a great time at the wedding, and I am sure they did. The wedding took place in Canton, Massachusetts, and Kathy's uncle, Father Leo, officiated over the ceremony.

Right up until the last minute, Kathy was nervous over whether or not I would actually show up for the wedding. She should have been, as Johnny and I dressed in full military uniform stopped at my dad's old watering hole, Mike Burn's Inn for a celebratory drink. Getting out of there was a challenge as everyone wanted to buy their favorite rubbish man and Marine a drink! We managed to escape and showed up just in the nick of time. The wedding went off without incident.

KATHY AND I CUTTING OUR WEDDING CAKE ON 4 NOVEMBER 1967

* * *

Kathy and I returned to Camp Lejeune after our honeymoon in Florida and shortly thereafter, I was deployed for six months to Guantanamo Bay (Gitmo).

At the time, tensions between the U.S. and Cuba were high, so the U.S. kept infantry and artillery units down there to deter any possible aggression directed at the base by Cuba. I was down there with the artillery battery while Kathy remained at Camp Lejeune. Those six months were uneventful but wild because, by some act of fate, John Prickett was down there, as well. [I would later in my career return to Gitmo as commander of a joint task force (JTF).]

CHAPTER 13

Decision Time

"The military life, whether sailor, soldier, or airman, is a good life, the human qualities it demands include fortitude, integrity, self-restraint, personal loyalty to other persons, and the surrender of the advantage of the individual to the common good. This is good company. Anyone can spend his life in it with satisfaction." --Sir John William Hackett

1968—1970

BOSTON, MASSACHUSETTS

Shortly after returning from Gitmo, I received orders to the Marine Barracks in Boston as the guard officer in command of Marines who were responsible for manning the gates for the security of the Charlestown Naval Shipyard. I also had the additional duty as a casualty assistance officer, and it turned out to be the hardest job of all.

The late 60s and early 70s saw a country in turmoil. Protests over the war were not confined to college campuses but were also found in most major cities around the country to include Boston and Washington, D.C. Vietnam was going full force, and the Marines were right in the middle of the action which resulted in me being quite busy with that collateral duty. I would go to the homes of Marines' families, accompanied by a chaplain, to notify them that their son or daughter had been wounded, was missing, had been killed in action or died from non-combat injuries. You never knew what the family's reaction would be as the reactions covered the spectrum from quiet acceptance, to anger, to disbelief, to unbelievable emotional outbursts. Nothing prepared you for such a task and, to this day, I remember each Marine and each family visit. It was a terrible, heart-wrenching job and through it, I knew how it must have been for the families, and loved ones of those men lost at Getlin's Corner.

My Boston tour lasted nearly two years. In 1969, before that tour ended, Kathy gave birth to our first child, Andrew, at Chelsea Naval Hospital. The very same hospital I visited as a casualty assistance officer and also where I spent a great deal of time checking on our wounded Marines.

Our time in Boston at the Barracks was instructive; those two years allowed us to enjoy and participate in all of Kathy's family activities, something we had not been able to do while at Camp Lejeune. And we enjoyed every moment of it. Summertime was particularly enjoyable and that second summer after our son Andrew was born we rented a cottage in Hull and spent quality time boating, going to the beach and socializing with family and friends.

It was a time where I wondered and really considered 'what's next' as far as the future was concerned. Though my responsibilities as a casualty assistance officer kept my mind on the war and the many newspaper articles on it did the same, I could feel that the war and the Marines engaged in it were losing their importance to the general public. Few people discussed it anymore and, except for close friends, few cared that I had served in Vietnam and was still a Marine.

My tour in Boston turned out to be the perfect litmus test for my career aspirations. I had looked around and explored other means of livelihood in the region where we wanted to live. I wasn't really attracted to what our family and friends were doing to earn a living in Boston, and that might have been part of the impetus to stay in the Marines.

I knew I could easily find a job, but the lure of the Corps and my Marines was ever-present in my thoughts. I had a nagging feeling that would not go away, a feeling that I had more to give. I felt that I still owed something to those Brothers I had served with and lost three years before. There was no doubt in my mind about job satisfaction. I liked being around the young men and women I served with, and I was good at training, mentoring and leading them.

Without a doubt, Kathy and I would be happy staying in the Boston area but I had my doubts that I would find the same job satisfaction I had with my Marines and the Corps. I was sure that I would not. This led to a serious discussion with Kathy and thankfully she agreed with my desire to stay in the Corps; I believe she knew better than I, the internal torment I lived with daily thinking of what had happened on 30-31 March 1967.

This was not an easy decision, and it tested the strength of our marriage and our love. I now had a wife and a new born son and considering the current fighting in Vietnam, it was almost a given that I would soon be going back if I stayed in the Corps. Knowing that my tour in Boston would soon be ending, I had made a request to my monitor (the individual at Marine Corps Headquarters who made personnel assignments) that if an opening occurred, I would like to be assigned as an infantry battalion advisor to the Vietnamese Marine Corps. The U.S. provided advisors, called Covans, down to the battalion level to aid and assist the Vietnamese Marines in training, tactics and operational planning. A fellow Marine and mentor had suggested that I request such a tour. It wasn't long before an opportunity presented itself and I was on my way back to Vietnam as an advisor.

Without a doubt, when I decided to return to Vietnam for the second tour, my lot was cast. The Marine Corps was my profession.

After all, Andrew was four months old when I left, and I wouldn't see him again until he was seventeen months old. Who in their right mind would leave their wife, young son, family, and friends and go away for thirteen months to war if they had not decided it was what they wanted as a career?

In my case, the deciding factor—the defining moment where all things are weighed and balanced—was the actions at Getlin's Corner. I had experienced uncommon valor and an unvarnished loyalty and dedication from and to my Marines. It was one of those seminal moments when I realized that those Marines looked to me for orders and most importantly, leadership. I had never before—at such a bone deep level—felt the level of trust they were placing in me. They trusted that I would get them through that battle or die trying. That sense of responsibility became part of me from that day forward. That essence of trust those men exuded toward me was something I wanted to continue to earn, and live up to, for as long as I was given the opportunity.

CHAPTER 14

BACK TO VIETNAM | BATTALION ADVISOR

"There is no more noble occupation in the world than to assist another human being." --Alan McGinnis

1970—1971

VIETNAM

NOTHING TO REPORT

The Marine Advisory Unit Headquarters was located in Saigon, so I flew directly there, checked in with the unit, and then into the hotel where the advisory unit had secured rooms. These were mostly used for storage of our personal gear we would not be taking with us into the field. I would only be traveling with what was on my back once I left Saigon.

There were perhaps 30 or 40 advisors in the Marine Advisory Unit at any one time, and we were each assigned to separate battalions and regiments in the Vietnamese Marine Corps. From my vantage point, I felt very fortunate in having the opportunity to work with and learn from such a team of professionals. Our activities were similar to what would occur with an ordinary U.S. Marine infantry outfit. My Vietnamese colleagues would receive orders from on high about the operations they were to conduct, and we would then work together in developing a plan. My counterparts were good commanders who knew their tactics, understood maneuver and never hesitated to take action. After all, most of them had been fighting for years and would continue fighting long after we left.

BEHIND THE WIRE WITH CAPTAIN TOM DRAUDE

During my first tour in Vietnam, I was young and getting my first taste of combat, just like all the junior officers I worked with at that time. I probably had every intention of returning to civilian life when I completed my four years of service. On this tour, however, all the officers, including me, were professionals—career officers—who had already experienced combat and had made the decision to stay in the Marine Corps.

I left my gear at the hotel and went to meet the man I'd be relieving—Tom Draude, a highly decorated Marine infantry captain. He passed on to me information, tricks of the trade, and anything else he thought I might need to be an effective infantry battalion advisor. Of critical importance were his efforts to ensure that the Vietnamese colonel, the battalion commander, and I were comfortable with each other.

Because I was urgently needed there, I didn't have the opportunity to first attend Vietnamese language school. Fortunately, the colonel spoke some English and French, and I spoke passible French, so we never really had a problem communicating.

I was there to live with the Vietnamese Marines, train with them, and operate with them wherever they might be assigned. It was just me—one Marine advisor with a radio, moving, shooting and communicating with and for them. They provided me with a young but savvy enlisted Vietnamese Marine—we affectionately called 'Cowboy'—who functioned as my assistant, helping carry the radio and other equipment we needed to survive during extended field operations.

As for food, I ate whatever the battalion commander ate. We were in this together and whatever was good enough for him was good enough for me. In fact, each month, I gave him money for food which, combined with his, allowed us to purchase locally produced rice and vegetables when they could find it in the marketplace, and a lot of scrawny chickens. It was important that we, as advisors, adopted and adapted to their lifestyle, customs and culture as much as possible. The building of trust and acceptance begins with these types of small gestures.

I will always remember my first Vietnamese holiday and the enormous fish they carted out as part of the celebration. Lord only knows where they got that huge fish. It was customary to let the guest—me—have the honor of eating the eyeballs. I couldn't very well decline such an honor so, even though it was a little dicey, I simply held my breath and let them slide down my throat.

I am blessed with a cast-iron stomach so during most of my tour as an advisor I had few problems. There was nothing I could do about the food and I liked it for the most part. But whether or not I liked the food, I had to be a gracious guest because I was essentially eating dinner in their home. On those occasions when field mice were served as the meat of the day, as they often were, they literally curled my intestines. Luckily, I had managed to *procure* some Scotch whiskey for just such occasions and gave it to the battalion commander as a gift. The hidden agenda was that it would assist us both in our digestive processes when faced with dubious meals.

I didn't see the other advisors too often, but when we were able to get together, the sharing of insights and lessons learned was invaluable. Becoming integrated into and learning from a group of some of the best infantry officers in the Marine Corps was the best part of the assignment. Many of them went on to become generals.

As an advisor, I operated in remote areas most of the time so felt even more strongly the pangs of being separated from my wife and son. We did not have the technology we have today that allows everyone to stay connected with the touch of a button. I usually gave any helicopter flying in support of us my mail and the same was true for receiving mail. [One time, my uncle sent me a little box that emitted laughter when you pushed a button. I liked to get on the radio and transmit that series of laughs just to cheer up my fellow advisors.]

There was always a two-to-three-week lag time before Kathy received my letters and the same was true of hers. Most times they came in bunches, and she and I used a numbering system so as to read them in some kind of order. I know the interval had a tremendous effect on her, as she never really knew where I was or how I was doing.

We moved and maneuvered as one outfit, and when I say moved I'm not kidding. We covered a lot of ground on that tour, moving from one end of Vietnam to the other.

In May, we received orders to expand operations into Cambodia. We boarded small boats and traveled up the Mekong River in accordance with the U.S. decision to uncover it as a safe haven for enemy forces. Much of our work to support that effort, however, was airborne.

LITTLE BIRD DOWN

I was fortunate on many occasions to have an Air Calvary (AirCav) package assigned to me for the conduct of operations. It was usually comprised of a mix of U.S. Army helicopters, including a command and control (C&C) helicopter, two light observation helicopters (referred to as Little Birds), two to four gunships and typically six UH-1N utility helicopters (Slicks) for transporting troops. Basic operations with the AirCav package was that my Vietnamese colleague and I would control events from the C&C helicopter and use the Little Birds to fly low to spot the enemy or to draw their fire to determine the enemy's location. Then, using the gunships to provide fire support, we would land troops close by and engage the enemy.

Using the helicopters in this fashion we discovered a mind-boggling number of weapons and equipment stacked and stored throughout the area. We would either recover them or destroy them in place. [As a token of my appreciation, I kept some of the weapons and gave them to pilots of aircraft that would stop to pick up letters I wanted to mail or if they were dropping off mail to me.] It was obvious that Cambodia was serving as a military warehouse for the enemy and thus was considered a wise move by us while back in the states the protests against it were enormous.

One particular day, some fixed-wing naval aircraft happened to be flying in the same vicinity and contacted me on my radio, requesting permission to drop ordinance on a village from which they said they had received fire. I asked them to show me where the fire had come from, and they literally indicated that it had come from the entire village. I wasn't about to let them drop bombs at random hoping that they managed to eliminate the threat. I denied their request and elected to run my Little Birds through the suspected area to see if we could determine the location of the enemy.

I advised my Vietnamese partner. "I'm going to have the Little Birds do a low but high-speed run along the river astride the village to see what we can flush out." He nodded, and I got on the radio with the Little Bird pilots. "Make a low pass following the middle of the river next to the village."

It was only a minute into their run when the roof of a village house opened up. Hidden under it was a manned anti-aircraft gun that immediately tracked the light helos and began firing. "Shit, both Little Birds are hit; one's headed into the water!" I tapped the pilot as I issued orders, "Turn the gunships loose on that AA gun!"

"Got it," he replied. "They're inbound; there's a lot of fire coming from several locations."

"Tell them to pile it on." I was scanning the area around the downed helo.

The pilot half-turned his head toward me. "You gonna land the Slicks with the troops?"

I was concerned about things getting out of hand. I didn't know what was on the ground and didn't want to get them down only to be encircled or cut-off. "No, too risky! Land next to where that one crashed." Leaning forward I pointed through the Plexiglas windscreen though the C&C pilot had seen where it went down, too.

He called over his shoulder to me. "We going after the crew?" We started taking fire, and that question never got answered. We exchanged a look, and both of us knew that we were not going to leave them. My thoughts flashed back to Hill 70 and fighting our way toward the India 3/9 command post, just three years before.

"I'll try to get them out; tell your door gunner to lay down covering fire and keep it coming." I switched channels and directed the gunships accompanying us, "Hit those enemy positions hard and keep pouring it on them and any others that pop up." My pilot nodded, gave them time to move in and then turned us straight into the zone where the ground fire was heaviest. They wanted those downed airmen. We weren't going to let that happen.

"Standby, I'm headed in. The bush near them looks heavy; I can't sit us down in that."

"Just get as close as you can." We were just feet off the ground over a semi-clear area. "I see one of them at the river's bank; the other one's still in the water struggling."

We landed one hundred meters from the downed Little Bird. "Keep the gunships over us to provide suppressing fire."

"Will do," the pilot nodded.

I took off my headset, jumped out and ran toward the pilots. The underbrush was tough to run through, further complicated by the swampy conditions and the increasing volume of enemy fire. Once they realized where we were and what we were doing, they really laid it on. When I reached the river bank, I found the observer had pulled himself onto the bank, while the more seriously hurt pilot, was still in the water. I fished him out and got the wounded pilot up on my shoulders and in a stumbling run made it back to my command helicopter. With the help of a crewman, I lifted him in. The observer had already limped toward us—making slow progress in closing the distance—and I dashed to help him. During both trips to the fallen airmen, bullets flew, but the gunships had done their job in making the enemy duck for cover or run to escape the hail of machine gun fire from them. Once again, I was lucky just as I was with John Prickett in the Battle of Getlin's Corner. Fortunately, neither of the injured airmen was seriously injured.

We got the hell out of there and dropped off the wounded airmen at an aid station. We took off and shortly thereafter landed to stage for the night. We hadn't been there long when another C&C helicopter landed. Out jumped a clean and well turned-out colonel who came looking for me.

"Are you the one who cost me one of my helicopters?" he screamed.

"Yes, sir." I faced him. "I'm Captain Neal and had an air cav package assigned to me when it happened." I could see him puffing, about to blast me again. I attempted to head that off. "I used the Little Birds for the very reason they were assigned to me, to identify enemy locations. I'm sorry we lost one helo and damaged another."

"You're sorry!" he sounded disgusted with me. "I could've lost a pilot and an observer. Did that enter your mind before you used them the way you did?"

It had. "Sir, I used them for the purpose they were intended." I felt confident in my actions but wasn't sure what his reaction was going to be.

He looked at me for a moment and shook his head. "You're right, captain. I agree with your reason for using the Little Birds." He seemed to relax a bit. "I do want to thank you, as do the two airmen, for risking your life to save them. Both are fine and will be back flying soon."

Much later, when I was back at the Advisory Headquarters during a break in operations, the deputy commander, Colonel Alexander McMillan, also known as 'Jaws' for his impressive ability to chew people out, called me in his office.

"Butch, anything of significance happen during your last operation?"

I responded "No sir, pretty routine," though I had a queasy feeling that by the way he was asking the question he already knew something; I felt the jaws closing in!

"I guess losing a helicopter and having another one damaged is no big deal to you, huh?"

"That colonel reported the incident to you?" He didn't answer me. "I thought he accepted my explanation and it was case closed sir."

"Case closed! Loss of one helo, damage to another, and two men injured and you stand there and say that!"

I could see this was going downhill in a hurry so I just went silent, expecting the worst. He rose from his desk, all six plus feet of him, and came around and grabbed me by the shoulders, screaming, "you little shit, the colonel just sent in a write up nominating you for at least the Silver Star and the best you can do is go mute on me!"

He had really fooled me. Until that last outburst, I had no clue he was really pleased with my actions and happy about the award recommendation.

* * *

Since we were on the move all the time, the thirteen-month tour passed quickly. Fortunately, there were not too many more instances such as that involving the downed pilots. In moving throughout Vietnam and into Cambodia we did engage the enemy on multiple occasions and each and every time I was amazed at how professional and offensive-minded the Vietnamese Marines were. As needed, I got them air support and assisted my counterpart with operational planning. He was a fearless leader and a true warfighter. And I learned much from him during that tour.

But for the fact that I had a wife and young son back home I would've elected to stay with the battalion for the duration. For me, personally, it was a lonely and challenging but ultimately rewarding tour; I had no regrets.

CHAPTER 15

COMING HOME (ONCE MORE)

"Learning without thought is labor lost; thought without learning is perilous." --Confucius

1971—1973

It was winter 1971 when I returned home. Kathy and Andrew picked me up from Boston's Logan Airport, and she immediately noticed I'd lost a lot of weight. Funny enough, while I was away, Kathy and I had met in Hawaii and spent ten days together, and *she* had lost so much weight that I didn't recognize her when I met her at the airport. I walked right past her. In her case, the weight loss was due to the stress of our separation and the constant worry for my safety. In my case, the weight loss was probably due to my Vietnamese diet.

Andrew was four months old when I left for Vietnam, and I had missed thirteen months of his infancy. Kathy had brought video footage of him for me to view during our Hawaii reunion since I had not had any other opportunities to see either of them during my Vietnam tour. Every reel was the little guy, learning to walk. We had some laughs while watching it because, in each reel, he would take a few steps and then tumble over.

Kathy had rented a house on the beach for my homecoming, and it was covered with snow when we arrived, a far cry from the climate I had experienced only 24 hours prior. The house was located on the south shore of Boston, close enough to my hometown that our relatives could come and visit us. We drove down there with no great plans except for us to enjoy each other, and for Andrew and me to have the time to get reacquainted.

[Not too long after I returned home from Vietnam, Andrew started calling me Guy. Later, when Andrew's sisters were born, they followed suit and the name stuck. To this day, that's what all three kids call me, and the grandkids call me Grandpa Guy. I kiddingly told everyone that the reason my kids started calling me Guy was because men would visit Kathy while I was away and the kids wanted to make sure they didn't call me by the wrong name. A funny story connected to all this occurred when Andrew and his playmates were playing soccer in our backyard, and I overheard my son referring to me as Guy. Soon, his friends all started referring to their dads as 'guy.' One would say something, and another would say, "Well, *my* guy..." It really tickled me, but my other nickname hadn't set well with me—at first. Years before, my grandmother had started calling me her little Butchie and the name stuck. I tried to change it to Richie in college, but it didn't take, probably because I was a commuter who spent more time in my hometown than at college, and everyone knew me as Butch. Today, any time I am invited to speak somewhere, the invitation is addressed to General Richard 'Butch' Neal.]

AMPHIBIOUS WARFARE SCHOOL (STUDENT)
QUANTICO, VIRGINIA

After leave in Boston, Kathy, Andrew and I headed to my next duty station. I was to attend Amphibious Warfare School (AWS), a six-month school for young captains from all branches of the military. It was the perfect tour to follow Vietnam, as I was able to have a great time with my family, relaxing and enjoying each other's company. I also got to mix and mingle with two hundred of my contemporaries.

We lived on base in prefab housing built during World War II or the Korean War. (We were given a housing allowance by the government, but since we lived in on-base housing, we forfeited it.) All the houses in the neighborhood were occupied by other students, and we never wanted for things to do. Living in houses with metal walls was interesting and challenging. In order to even hang a picture, you needed an electric drill with a metal bit. And one of our best friends, Bill Murphy, who was a fellow Bostonian and classmate, gave us car polish as a gag gift, suggesting that we could use it to keep the walls clean.

The real beauty of AWS is that it provided us with the opportunity to study our profession while at the same time build relationships and professional reputations with other officers from the Marine Corps, the other services, and several international students. While there, they had a ceremony during which I was awarded my second Silver Star for the action in Cambodia. Most, if not all of the students at AWS had spent at least one tour in Vietnam, so there were a lot of decorated combat vets in the class.

But the war was winding down at this time, and the Marine Corps was already looking at policies that would allow them to reduce the size of the force. In this environment, there was still a sense of relief that we had made it home safely.

I'm sure that my second award came into play shortly thereafter when I got nominated for what could be a political hot potato; an out of the ordinary assignment that had to be completed successfully.

BACK TO HIGH SCHOOL

At the end of six months at AWS, I thought I was going to be reassigned to TBS, where I'd gone as a lieutenant to teach tactics to the new lieutenants. From my point of view, this was a perfect assignment where I could engage with the young lieutenants and share my experiences and hopefully prepare them for combat. I was excited, but at the eleventh hour, I received a call from my monitor in the Officer Assignment Branch and the conversation went something like this:

"Hey Butch, sorry to pull you out of class but wanted to know if you'd like to be assigned to New Orleans."

I didn't like where this conversation seemed to be headed. "No way, why would you want to send a Yankee down there? I'm excited about going to TBS."

"You may not have a choice. We just got a direct requirement from the commandant's office to fill a position down there, no questions asked."

I let some of my consternation show in my voice. "What billet's that important?"

"Stay calm. You'd be commanding a Junior Reserve Officer Training Corps (JROTC) unit at Jesuit High School in New Orleans."

"You gotta be kidding! I thought those were run by retired officers and enlisted."

"Ordinarily they are, but this was the first Marine Corps JROTC in the country. And right now, it's in trouble and could be thrown out of the school or pulled by the Marine Corps. It's high visibility and important people including the Commandant of the Marine Corp (CMC) don't want that to happen. They've decided to send an active duty captain down to hopefully salvage the program."

"Why me? I could better use my experience to help prepare young lieutenants for combat."

"No argument, but you have a degree in education, are Catholic, and readily available." His tone told me this was a done deal despite him opening the conversation as if I had a say in it. "So I need you to report to Headquarters Marine Corps tomorrow in your dress green uniform. From there you'll be taken to Capitol Hill to meet Louisiana Congressman F. Edward Hebert, who is the Chairman of the House Armed Services Committee—one of the most powerful committees as far as the military is concerned. Now you know why this is high vis!"

The next day there I was a young captain on Capitol Hill, walking through the halls of Congress for the very first time. I was taken into Congressman Hebert's spacious office and introduced to him. In addition to being the Chairman, he was considered the father of the JROTC Program, a distinction of which he was very proud. This program, supported by the individual services, was offered in high schools nationwide and was viewed as a valuable course that emphasized leadership, citizenship, and individual responsibility.

Chairman Hebert was also a proud graduate of Jesuit High School in New Orleans and he was especially delighted by the fact that the Marine Corps was in his high school. At the time, there was a World War II veteran running the program and, for various reasons, the program was suffering from poor enrollment and low prestige. Obviously, Congressman Hebert did not want this to happen and, given his position as chairman and controller of the purse strings, he had the power to ask the Commandant of the Marine Corps to fix things.

So, I had been selected to be the fixer. During my interview, Congressman Hebert asked me a lot of questions about my career. He had a printout of my record and was most interested in the March 30—31st battle, the heroics of those involved and pointedly about my actions concerning the downed airmen in Cambodia. Finally, he stood up and said to me in a soft Southern accent, "Well, son, I think you're gonna be just *fine.*" Then he reached into his desk draw, pulled out his Jesuit High School yearbook and passed it to me, saying, "Take this and get the Jesuit Bluejay spirit!"

That was that, as far as he was concerned. He notified the commandant of his desire to have me assigned as the Senior Military Instructor for Jesuit high School. That meant I wouldn't be headed to TBS as a tactics instructor where I would share what I had learned at AWS with the new lieutenants; that would have to wait. After signing out of AWS and making arrangements to move our furniture and other personal effects, Kathy and I loaded the car and headed to New Orleans with Andrew in the back seat. I had no idea how this assignment would turn out. Would I be challenged or bored stiff? Would I dislike the students or, worse, would the faculty resent a young, active duty, Marine landing on their doorstep? My brain was buzzing with these questions all the way from Quantico to New Orleans.

* * *

NEW ORLEANS

I shouldn't have worried because right from the start we loved the school, the people, the town and the food so much, we both would have been perfectly happy to stay there until we were old and gray. We bought our very first house in the town of Gretna, Louisiana, located about five miles across the river from New Orleans and Jesuit High School.

[Throughout my Marine Corps career, we would buy not only this home in Louisiana but three in Northern Virginia, one in Florida and one in Washington, D.C. As a military family, when we needed to move, we never had the luxury of time being on our side; time to wait for the right buyer who met our selling price. This became particularly important when our family grew to three small children. We were always anxious to get to our new assignment so that we could get the kids settled in time for the start of school. The combination of these factors often put us in a position where we had to accept less money when we sold our homes than we might have gotten had we been able to wait it out. The same was true when we bought a new house. We always tried to buy nice homes in a good school district but never had the leisure to shop around or negotiate the best price. I used to jokingly brag that I had gotten home buying down to a fine science: buy high, sell low.]

I decided that, while we were in New Orleans, I would pursue my master's degree at Tulane University, so once I figured out my work schedule at Jesuit High School, I enrolled. In addition to my academic pursuits and achievements, I was given credit for some of my accomplishments and training while in the Marine Corps. I worked hard and, blessed with Kathy as my typist, I was able to receive my Master's Degree in Education during my two-year tour.

At that time, I was the only active duty officer ever to run a JROTC program, and it was a great experience. The young men in the program were all volunteers, and they looked forward to the classes, the drill, and the trips. I was also blessed with the support of a great principal and friend, Mike Powers, and was ably assisted by two retired enlisted Marines who were just terrific. MSgt. Cresseonne and MSgt. Cappell were loved and respected by the students and the faculty. We had a great time working together. Our Cadet Corps was once again proud to wear the uniform, and the school loved our terrific drill team and our first-class band. Unbelievably, we were named the number one Marine Corps JROTC in the country. When the inspector general paid a visit to inspect the unit, he and his team were impressed with the turnaround of the unit and the excitement and *esprit de corps* of the young men.

You might ask how we went from almost being thrown out or pulled out of the school to being number one in the country. It was just a common-sense approach to leadership. We showed respect for the students while at the same time making sure that they understood our expectations of them and letting them know what they could expect from us. And that is eyeball level leadership at its finest.

It was time for me to get back to the Marine Corps; the monitor kept his word of this being only a two-year assignment and that summer we received orders to Camp Lejeune, North Carolina. When we left Jesuit High School, we had a new addition to our family, our first daughter, Amy Elizabeth and her godparents were Mike and Shirley Powers.

MY SON ANDREW WATCHES ME DURING A CEREMONY AT JESUIT HIGH SCHOOL

CHAPTER 16

POSTWAR CHALLENGES

"Coming together is a beginning; keeping together is progress; working together is success." --Henry Ford

1973–1975

CAMP LEJEUNE, NORTH CAROLINA

FRESH AIR AT LAST (BUT)

Reporting to Camp Lejeune after spending two years at Jesuit High School was an eye-opening experience. The Marine Corps I knew and loved was in serious trouble; racial violence, drugs and crime were more the norm than the exception throughout the base. Discipline, attention to duty, and pride of being a Marine were missing.

A lot of Marines returning from Vietnam found the slow pace of peacetime, with all of its rules and regulations, difficult to adjust to. This was not the challenging, active life they had envisioned (and grown accustomed to) when they joined or were drafted. Many, if given the choice, would prefer to just go home.

The Marine Corps, as well as the other services, was in the throes of transitioning from a warfighting posture, after years in Vietnam, to a peacetime force. Not only was the draft ended and the all-volunteer force implemented, but we were also in the process of winding down from a very unpopular war. As is usual at such times, military budgets were cut resulting in fewer dollars for training, educating and maintaining the force.

It was into this environment that I arrived as the Executive Officer (XO) for 5th 175-mm Gun Battery, and soon had my hands full with disciplinary problems. As the executive officer, I had the opportunity to talk with all of the Marines in the battery, and they were an unhappy lot. The most telling example of low morale that I witnessed was the number of Marines being disciplined. I would come into work in the morning and see lines of them outside the commander's office awaiting punishment for offenses ranging from unauthorized absence, to use of drugs, to desertion.

It wasn't unusual for me to see Marines who no longer even cared what they looked like. But there were good Marines, too. The good Marines were mostly those fresh out of boot camp or those who had made the decision to stay in for perhaps a career. Their almost universal concerns and complaints were centered on what they rightfully saw as the focus being almost exclusively on the bad Marines. As they saw it, the leadership spent the majority of their time disciplining the bad to the exclusion of training and leading the good.

Boy, were they right! Walking through the squad bays where the Marines slept and kept their personal gear was at times scary. All of the Marines being disciplined hung out in the squad bay awaiting punishment while the good Marines were out doing normal battery activity with half the manpower. Bottom line, the good worked while the bad loafed, a toxic environment if there ever was one. On more than one occasion I can remember grabbing a disorderly or disrespectful Marine and threatening him with physical abuse if he didn't shape up. Was this wrong? You bet, but at that time in our Corps, such measures were, unfortunately, more routine than I would have liked.

I remember one occasion when walking through the barracks I found a Marine stretched out on his rack in the middle of the day. I stopped and asked him, "What are you doing here, instead of at the gun park with your unit?"

"I'm waiting on office hours and hope to be thrown out of your green machine!"

He didn't get off his bunk and didn't even look up at me. That set me off. "Well until you do, get off your ass and stand at attention when addressing an officer, understand?" I leaned over him to emphasize my point.

"Come on captain, don't play chicken shit with me, I already had a Summary Court Martial and will probably get a Special at office hours. I don't need you harassing me!"

I reached over and grabbed him by the collar and yanked him out of the rack with one hand and stood him against the wall with my other hand on his throat. "You may get a Special at office hours, but then again you may not live to make it there because I've a good mind to beat the living shit out of you! You understand me?!"

He happened to be about 5'10" to my 5'6" but I think my quick action had completely caught him off guard and put the fear of God in him. There was nothing but "Yes Sir, No Sir" out of him from that point on. As I walked out of the squad bay, I thought of my fifteen Marine brothers lost in Vietnam and about what they would have thought of what I had just done. Would they be disappointed in our Corps or in me?

Another day, a particularly devastating event occurred that is worthy of mentioning and a *What Now, Lieutenant?* moment I would not soon forget. While sitting in my office conducting a counselling session with one of my Marines, I heard someone shouting in the hallway "Call an ambulance!" I rushed out and was directed to the head (bathroom) where I found a Marine lying on the floor, convulsing. In his hand, he had a cardboard spool on which toilet paper is normally wrapped and inside it was paper. He had been spraying the deodorant Right Guard into one end and sniffing the other end to get high.

There were no cries for "Corpsman up" or Corporal Loweranitis running around defending his fellow Marines on Hill 70.

There were no life-saving heroics; no 'we-don't-leave-any-man-behind' ethos that could help. Here we had the tragic circumstance of a Marine accidentally killing himself. Here we had the beginning of the process where some officer near this Marine's home of record would make a casualty call to tell the Marine's wife and his parents that her husband and their son was dead. Harder still had to be telling them how it happened.

This was not the Marine Corps I had signed up for, and this was not how I envisioned losing a Marine. The confluence of such events, situations and issues resulted in the leadership spending most of our time dealing with these problems instead of spending time training and leading the good Marines. It was probably the closest I ever came to leaving the service.

At this low point in our Marine Corps, we welcomed the arrival of a new commandant, General Louis Wilson. He was a World War II Medal of Honor recipient and wasn't about to let his Marine Corps flounder any longer. He set about to make some changes. His attitude was, "I don't care if we end up with only two Marines in the Marine Corps—me and the sergeant major! I am not about to sacrifice what the Marine Corps is all about just to keep our numbers up. We need to get rid of all these folks who are giving us problems and no longer want to be Marines!"

Wow! Up until that point in time, it was very difficult to kick Marines out. You had to jump through many legal hoops to make it happen. There also had been a feeling that the Marine Corps couldn't fall below a certain number—that we had to keep those numbers up in order to be ready. But General Wilson believed that was irrelevant if the Corps was not made up of good Marines. He was unwilling to place manpower strength ahead of quality. He initiated what would come to be known as the Expeditious Discharge Program, allowing us to bypass a lot of those legal encumbrances that held up the process. This enabled us to administratively release Marines who were counterproductive to the good order and discipline expected of Marines. As a result of his initiative, it felt as if someone had opened a window to let in fresh air. Now we could focus on training, mentoring and leading only those who really wanted to be Marines.

[As you know by now, I'd been a firm believer in eyeball level leadership since Getlin's Corner. I had always considered it essential to get to know the people under my command and to learn details like where they came from, whether they were single or married, and what problems they might be facing. These are things you can only know by engaging with them. I learned a lot walking through the squad bay and joining the Marines in the mess hall at five o'clock in the morning to ensure that the food was ready for them and adequate in quantity and quality. Showing that you care. Those actions are what good leadership is all about.]

The new and refreshing command climate caused me to jettison any ideas I had of leaving the Corps. Shortly thereafter, I was given command of my own firing battery, 2nd 155 Howitzers. The benefits of the Expeditious Discharge program became even more pronounced to me now that I had assumed command of a battery filled with Marines who understood, subscribed to, and embraced what it meant to be a Marine. Retaining only those who really wanted to be in the Corps made it a pleasure for me to lead them and returned to me the job satisfaction that had previously begun to wane.

The battery was one of three howitzer batteries recently added to the 10th Marine Regiment—and it was an exciting time. Most of the young Marines sent to me had recently joined the Marine Corps so they were not the kind with problems, veterans who wanted out of the Marine Corps. These were young men, excited about being Marines. They brought with them more fresh air.

Everything I received was brand new, and we built it from the ground up with the people assigned to me. We wrote all the training, maintenance and standard operating procedures for the organization. We were in friendly but fierce competition with one of the other new batteries, and its commander, Gary Blair. He and I were forever jousting as to which battery was best; *Second to None* was our battle cry and my Marines lived up to it.

Chapter 17

A Marine Between Wars

"Let us cherish, therefore the means of knowledge. Let us dare to read, think, speak and write. Let every sluice of knowledge be opened and set a-flowing." --John Adams

1975—1978
Washington, D.C.

I hated to give up command of 2nd 155 Howitzers and leave all those great Marines, but it was time to move on to a new assignment. I received Permanent Change of Station (PCS) orders and Kathy and I packed the car for a move to Northern Virginia. As we drove away, we had a new little passenger in the back seat with us. Erin was born while we were at Camp Lejeune and she was a wonderful addition to our family.

[I hadn't really thought about it before, but as I started putting this book together, I suddenly realized that after leaving Vietnam as an advisor in 1971 there would be twenty years before I went to war again. It was hard to think about those twenty years in that context, but it caused me to do some thinking about how to tell the rest of my story. Should I go on in a chronological fashion or should I focus on those things and events that stand out during that timeframe? I am opting for a little bit both. Before going there, it might prove interesting to cite a couple of data points: two years after my coming home from Vietnam the second time, in 1973, the military draft ended and our country went to an All-Volunteer Force. Two years later, in 1975, the Vietnam War officially ended. During the twenty years between wars I moved my family ten times, we added two daughters to our family, each of our children attended two high schools, and I had eleven different assignments. These events and circumstances serve as the underpinning for my journey between wars.]

I had been assigned to Headquarters Marine Corps in Washington, D.C. in the ground assignment section (monitor). Being the Company Grade assignment officer at headquarters, my team was responsible for assigning lieutenants and captains to billets around the Marine Corps. As in all my previous tours to date, I was fortunate to be working with a truly superb group of professionals, and I would learn much from them while establishing lifelong relationships. One of the highlights of the tour was the running community that met every morning at headquarters. We were all into running and pushed each other to do our best. Two of the three Marines I ran with went on to become general officers—Don Lynch became a two-star general, and Jack Sheehan became a four-star general. Then there was Fred Smith—not a Marine but a valued friend to us all, who had been in the Navy and was later selected for several high-level positions within the Department of Defense as a member of the Senior Executive Service (SES).

It was a good group. In the process of running together, we developed a camaraderie and during the runs, we would feed off the news of the day and the rumors we had heard. We had what we called the Five O'clock Rule, which meant what was discussed on a run, stayed on the run. It was a great time for us all and, although our best friend Fred died early, Jack and I still get together a couple of times a month for breakfast and Don, who settled back in Texas, stays in touch via e-mail.

During this time, we all got into running at a more serious level than ever before, and it all began with the establishment of the Marine Corps Marathon. I would end up running several Marine

Corps Marathons and, from the first to the last, my time in each was under three hours. I had the best time of all in the last marathon. I also ran the Boston Marathon twice which, as you can imagine, was the cause of great excitement among my wife and our relatives. For the first one they were waiting for me at the finish line with a laurel wreath for my head. It was a big event for everyone and cause for great celebration at Kathy's family home in South Boston. Both times I ran my time was under three hours.

FAMILY TIME DURING THE HOLIDAYS

While at Headquarters, I was nominated to be the Junior Military Aide to President Carter. At the White House to interview for the job, right from the outset I didn't see the appeal of the assignment or the working environment. More significantly, being away from the Marine Corps and my Marines, I would have become what is called in military parlance 'a horse holder.' [The term originated in olden days when an aide would hold the horse for the general, a position some might covet but not me.] I also knew that the demands of the assignment would have had an impact on my responsibilities as a husband and father. We now had three children, and I didn't care to sacrifice my time with them for a job I didn't even anticipate enjoying.

I experienced a mild sense of a *What Now, Lieutenant?* moment when I made the decision the next morning, while shaving, that it was not what I wanted to do. The problem was that if you were nominated for such a position and selected, you were expected to accept it. I fully realized that declining the position was a pretty bold move for a young major, but I was willing to accept whatever impact my decision might have on my future assignments and promotions. So that morning I told the Assistant Commandant that I didn't want the job. He took a long look at me and was quiet for a few moments. Then he said, "Well, major when I need a junior aide to replace my current one, you won't be given a choice!"

AIDE TO THE ASSISTANT COMMANDANT

Sure enough, not too long afterwards, I became the Aide to the Assistant Commandant for a year. I worked for General Sam Jaskilka, a great man, Marine, and leader. Of Ukrainian heritage, he graduated from the University of Connecticut, joined the Marine Corps and never looked back.

From the moment, I started as his aide it was great. He had a terrific sense of humor and quite frankly we were very much alike: decorated from our time in combat, we both liked to run, and we enjoyed being around Marines. He often called me Marmaduke (from the dog in the cartoon) because he was sure I was sitting at his desk when he was out.

I believe General Wilson, the commandant, chose him because he brought different strengths and capabilities to their leadership team. They essentially complimented each other. General Jaskilka had a greater appreciation for how to run the staff of the headquarters to make sure the commandant was well served. He had unusually good relations with those on Capitol Hill and with those within DOD.

I watched him and the commandant work the issues and was amazed at their common-sense approach to every challenge. The opportunity to see senior decision makers within the Corps tackle matters from the mundane to the most important was an education few had the opportunity to observe. It allowed me to better understand and to put into context how decisions were made at that level. I learned that most issues were not black or white (which up to that point was how I tended to view things). They were complex, and you had to think beyond the immediate and consider unintended consequences of each and every decision.

This assignment taught me there are instances when a gray approach is best. A commander must be able to view things with the lens wide open and take into consideration all relevant facts before making a decision. Thereafter, words such as extenuation and mitigation became a permanent part of my vocabulary and thought process.

[This experience served me well as I moved up the rank structure and had great utility when I served as General Krulak's Assistant Commandant of the Marine Corps (ACMC). Though the issues were very different, they still required the same intellectual rigor, assessment and focus so as to provide the best information from which the commandant could make a decision. One of the great things I learned from General Jaskilka was that you never got so senior that you forgot those who got you there, the young Marines you had the pleasure of working with. He taught me that lesson by example. He never failed to ask me "what do you think" after allowing me to review an issue requiring a decision.]

I was coming to the end of my tour as aide when the unthinkable happened, we had a house fire! Kathy called my office:

The Marine clerk answered and told her, "Ma'am, he's out running."

"You go find him and tell him our house is going up in flames!" Kathy went ballistic on him, "Tell him to get home immediately!"

It seemed that whenever John Prickett was around, I got in trouble. He had been up visiting us and Kathy had taken him to the airport only to return to find the house on fire. The firefighters were able to contain the blaze to the upper floor of our split-level home but the kitchen and most of the dining room were destroyed and the smoke damage throughout the top floor was substantial.

Fortunately, no one was hurt and with the bottom floor untouched we were able to live there. We rented a RV-trailer, parking it in the backyard, and it served as our temporary kitchen until the upstairs was repaired. Kathy, as always, made it happen through her unbelievable ability to adapt and to make the best out of a terrible situation.

It was during this time that I was selected to attend Command and Staff College in the fall.

MARINE CORPS COMMAND AND STAFF COLLEGE

This nine-month course of instruction was a great assignment for I would have the opportunity to learn from two hundred of my peers from all services—Army, Navy, Air Force, Coast Guard and, of course, my Marine Corps. Each officer brought different experiences, education, and expertise to the table. We also had about ten international students, including officers from Australia, the United Kingdom, Thailand and the Netherlands.

Similar to AWS, the class was broken into dens, and each was comprised of ten to fifteen members, with each service and an international student represented in each group. The groups stayed together for the nine months, and the curriculum consisted of a mixture of full class lectures, exercises, and small group discussions. During the course, we had many guest speakers, including all of the service chiefs as well as many noted authors, historians and civilian leaders from the Departments of Defense, State, and Justice.

It was a beneficial year and a rare opportunity to exchange real life experiences with people who had different experiences, expertise and views. We fed off each other's ideas, and the camaraderie was wonderful. The dens were also competitive in different athletic events throughout the school year, and we all enjoyed a friendly rivalry. The relationships established during those nine months were invaluable and, in all likelihood, graduates of this course would be working with or calling on their classmates for assistance or advice, even years down the line. In fact, that is the single most important aspect of attending any and all of these schools—the establishment of relationships that will be with you the rest of your career.

DRESSED FOR THE COMMAND AND STAFF COLLEGE MARINE CORPS BALL

The schoolhouse was an environment that naturally allowed you to either burnish or diminish your reputation. After all, here were military folks of the same rank from all services and other nations observing, engaging and listening to each other on a daily basis. Whether leading a team in problem solving or participating as a team member, it was impossible to hide or rest on past laurels. During the course, the true professionals stood out and were recognized as such. They were all top-flight people, and I learned a lot, not only from the formal instruction presented in the classroom environment but from the rich exchange of experiences and ideas down in the den. Significantly, our class was to yield the highest number of general officers in the years ahead, including the first female three-star general in the Marine Corps.

Chapter 18

Wing Exchange Tour on Okinawa

"Look beneath the surface, let not the several qualities of a thing nor its worth escape you." --Marcus Aurelius

1978—1979

There Are No Bad Assignments

The small size of the Marine Corps made it easy to gauge when an overseas deployment was imminent. Aside from short deployments while at Camp Lejeune, I hadn't really been away from my family since Vietnam so I knew I was due. I was given two options—to take an accompanied tour for three years overseas, or an unaccompanied tour for one year overseas. By now, we had three children, all in various stages of school. So, I opted to leave my family where they were outside of Quantico and in 1978, I flew to Okinawa to begin my one-year tour.

Wing Wiper for a Year

My tour on Okinawa was a true learning experience as it provided me with the opportunity to fully understand the inner workings of a Marine Aircraft Group (MAG), its people, its aircraft and how it all came together in the conduct of operations. While there, I learned aviation from A to Z and established great personal and professional relationships with a segment of the Marine Corps population I wouldn't normally have much interaction with except during exercises or in the schoolhouse. [At Camp Lejeune, for example, you have all the ground forces on the base while the aviation elements are spread between New River, Beaufort, and Cherry Point—locations completely separated from the ground organizations.]

MAG-36 was a composite group with an assortment of aircraft: C-130 transport planes, OV-10 aircraft, CH-53 heavy lift helicopters, CH-46 medium-lift helicopters, UH-1N utility helicopters, and AH-1 Cobra gunships. In my capacity as the assistant operations officer, I was working with the operations officer (S-3) responsible for all air operations and development of supporting air plans—all the nuts and bolts associated with Marine Corps aviation. I did have quite a bit of experience with air support (Air Cav Package) during my advisor tour and that familiarity, coupled with now actually planning for their employment, was an invaluable learning opportunity for me.

It was a perfect organization for my professional development as I learned everything about aviation in support of ground forces and got to learn how Marine Corps aviation worked to support that mission.

I was affectionately known as the 'Group Grunt,' a euphemism used for a ground officer working in an air assignment. They took great pleasure in teasing me about my being a ground hog. To ensure I felt at home, they provided me with a box of dirt so I would feel comfortable. Of course, I took great delight in ragging them about their appearance and military demeanor which on most occasions left a bit to be desired. What do I mean by this? Well, they were more relaxed and less formal and were accustomed to addressing each other using nicknames or first names instead of by rank and name. I found this informality refreshing, and you can bet I took full advantage of every opportunity to correct them:

Observing a captain violating one of the Corps' sacrosanct uniform regulations, I'd ask, "Are your hands cold, captain? I assume they must be since you have them in your pockets!"

"You need to introduce your boots to polish and your head to a barber when you have the opportunity!"

There was no shortage of such exchanges, and they made the tour that much more enjoyable. Ground officers called aviators 'Jet Jockeys' and 'Rotor Heads', but there was no question that they knew how to play hard; the Friday Night Happy Hours were always special (I recall waking up one Saturday morning on the lawn of the Officer's Club). The friendly competition between me, and each of them was unending. For instance, I challenged them to a physical fitness test, and though I couldn't beat a couple of their running rabbits, I was able to do the entire test (20 pull-ups, 80 sit ups and the 3-mile run) in under 19 minutes which bought me a lot of refreshments at Happy Hour.

Given the assortment of aircraft in the group, you can bet that the Group Grunt was not the only one being ragged on a continuous basis. It was also the helicopter pilots against the fixed-wing pilots and the gunship pilots against the transport helo pilots. It was fun to be a part of, and as the duty non-pilot, I got to switch sides as I saw fit. But the real takeaway from this assignment with MAG-36 was the absolute professionalism of the aviators. It is important to remember that flying is a dangerous endeavor in both peacetime and in combat. There are no days off, or shortcuts to flight safety and everyone knew it. From the pilots to the crewmen, to the maintenance folks; all worked together as a team to insure safety and mission success.

We non-aviators, regardless of MOS, have always viewed aviators as at least a notch below real Marines, those of us who fight the enemy up close and personal. They were almost too casual in their dealing with enlisted Marines, too relaxed in how they wore their uniform or kept up their personal appearance, and most assuredly, we knew they were not interested in anything beyond flying. My year living, laughing, and working with them disabused me of each of those impressions and perceptions. Sure, their approach to some things was different but at the end of the day, they wanted to accomplish the mission.

JUST FINISHED A HOP ON A COBRA GUNSHIP

It was hard to be separated from my family for a year. By that time, the kids were eight, six, and four years old. At least while I was away, the family got to stay in the same house we had lived in while I was at Command and Staff College. We stayed connected by phone and wrote letters back and forth, and I also brought a bunch of storybooks with me and read them onto cassettes for the kids. I had fun with it, embellishing every story and being somewhat theatrical in my readings. In this way, I made the stories seem more personal. I sent those cassettes home periodically, and the kids loved them.

I received my new orders about halfway through the tour and was surprised and pleased to learn I would be returning to AWS as an instructor. Around the same time, I was selected for lieutenant colonel, so in addition to being an instructor, I would be running the operations branch at the school.

CHAPTER 19

AMPHIBIOUS WARFARE SCHOOL (STAFF)

"Considering my pupils as members of the same family– almost as my own children–I think I feel nearly as deep an interest in their improvement, happiness and future welfare as do the parents themselves. If they have faults, it is my great object to reform them, if foibles, to correct them."

--Alden Partridge, Founder of Norwich University

1979—1983
QUANTICO, VIRGINIA

While I was gone, my family brought home a big black dog and gave him the unoriginal name of Blackie. I think Kathy had gotten the dog to take the kids' minds off my absence. Because I wasn't there when the family first brought Blackie home, when I showed up I was a stranger, and the dog understandably saw me as an invader of his territory. The dog took one look and decided he didn't like me. The feeling was mutual. Evidently, before I got home, he was sleeping on the bed with my wife. Now, all of a sudden, here was this guy he didn't know from Adam, shoving him off the bed. Needless to say, we did not exactly get along.

We had decided before I returned home to look at buying a new home in a development closer to Quantico, one that had good schools and the added advantage of a lake so the kids could swim. Fortunately, we found the perfect home in Montclair and were able to sell our present home in short order. As the moving day drew closer, I told Kathy "I'm not moving that dog!" Blackie and I still were at odds with each other, and there was no way he was coming with us to our new house. Well, lo and behold, while we were packing up the house on moving day, the dog just dropped dead. The timing of Blackie's demise was unplanned and shocking, Kathy and the kids were devastated. While Blackie and I never really hit it off, I felt bad at the suddenness of his death and the impact it had on the family.

ERIN AND BLACKIE

After the move and settling into our new home, we got another dog. Pepper was a true mutt: his mother was a Schnauzer and his father was from a 'good neighborhood.' He was my running buddy for the next 18 years.

* * *

Here I was in a schoolhouse again, only this time as head of the operations branch at AWS. I had five or six instructors working for me—all majors—and we were responsible for all instruction except ground operations. The quality of these instructors was phenomenal. They were experienced officers on the fast track for promotion. I had no problem putting them in front of two hundred captains to teach a class. They were experienced and confident, had a good grasp of their lesson plans and, through practice and rehearsal, improved and enhanced their instructional technique. It was a wonderful two years with quality instructors and top-notch students.

I now found myself in the role of den daddy which gave me the wonderful opportunity to experience that dynamic from the other side of the table. Instead of being one of the members of the den, I was now responsible for ensuring that the students understood and digested what they read, heard and saw in the classroom, during exercises and when on field trips. I served not only as a role model and mentor but also a facilitator for their professional development.

It was my job to squeeze all the goodness out of each of the officers so that they could share it with their classmates. I always seemed to have a good bunch of students with representatives from all of the services and at least one international officer. Typically, after classroom instruction or a day spent listening to a guest speaker, we would retire to the individual dens and I, as den daddy, would facilitate a discussion of what we had heard, seen, or participated in, as the case might be. I would help them put the instruction they had received in context so that it made sense, rather than leaving them to try to digest all the information on their own. Needless to say, we had lively discussions, and everyone benefitted from the exchange of ideas. Something we stressed throughout the academic year was the establishing of both personal and professional relationships not only with those in their den but also with all of their classmates. We emphasized that this year was a golden opportunity to learn from those with different backgrounds, specialties, cultures, and experiences; in many respects, we thought these relationships were as valuable as the classroom instruction.

On many occasions, we used the proximity of various Civil War battlefields to our advantage. We would have already studied the battle through assigned readings, and then as we walked the ground, I would talk them through it. In this way, we brought to reality what was on the page. For example, when touring Gettysburg, we would identify the main participants of the battle and then I'd ask questions such as;

"Now, what do you think General Longstreet thought of the plan of attack both before and during the battle?"

"Why do you suppose General Lee attacked when he did? Did he suffer from a lack of good intelligence?"

"How would the terrain influence the decisions you would have made?"

"What would you have done differently if you were in charge?"

These were the type of questions the students actually looked forward to; it was interactive leadership which brought history to life for them. It challenged them with a situation and mission, requiring them to think through what they would have done if faced with the same situation. These were true *What Now, Lieutenant?* moments that forced the students to incorporate their classroom instruction, experience, and common sense into a course of action to accomplish the mission. Mistakes were made but better in the classroom or on a field trip than in combat. It was as good as it gets for everyone concerned—the captains and the instructors.

A particular incident is probably worth sharing. One time, one of the dens had done something wrong—missed a class or been inattentive or something—and I really got angry. I called the members together and raised cane with them. I told them that they had acted in an unprofessional manner and were a real disappointment to me. I warned them that they had better clean up their act. I left them to contemplate and reflect upon my words and to discuss among themselves what I had said.

About half an hour later, I saw some of them in the hallway and acted as if nothing had occurred. The fact that the relationship seemed back to normal was a shock to them. This was one of the first times they had ever gotten chewed out without it having a carry-over effect. They had feared that I would be pissed for months on end and hold a grudge and that I might have lost confidence in them. They couldn't believe I would resume treating them as the professionals I knew them to be so shortly after the chewing out. My teaching point for them was one they fully grasped and appreciated.

My leadership style demanded I get their attention and respect right away. It was important that they turn themselves around. I found over the years that if you don't watch it, complacency can lead to contempt. It was equally important for me to then move on and make it clear that I accepted them for the high-quality people I knew them to be. Staying mad at them for an extended period of time would have served no purpose and actually could have been counterproductive. Having the opportunity to work with and hopefully influence the professional and personal development of these young men and women gave me great job satisfaction.

NATIONAL WAR COLLEGE

During my second year at AWS, I was selected to attend the National War College in Washington, D.C. Off came my instructor's hat and on went my student hat. This would be the last schoolhouse for me but, as we all know, our learning and education never stops. A Marine officer's profession is so dynamic because it is people intensive and there are always new leaders to adjust to, new doctrine introduced, new practices and procedures to absorb.

Without a doubt, each time I went to school the benefits were incredible. In addition to the lifelong relationships established with classmates from each school, each of the schools helped me grow professionally and personally. Being given the opportunity to attend a war college can best be described as frosting on the cake. As I've said, the Army, Navy, and National War Colleges take the entire experience up another couple of notches. They cover and discuss subjects at the strategic level.

I commuted daily with a great group of folks, including guys from the Secret Service and FBI. We were all mid-level executives-to-be who, by virtue of being selected for the National War College, had a good chance of eventual promotion to a higher rank or important positions within our respective services or organizations. You can imagine the dialogue and banter as we traveled daily up and down Highway 95. In many respects, the quality of the discussions matched the dialogue and banter of a den.

The makeup of the class was superb. We were broken up into study groups with representatives from each of the services, as well as civilians from the different departments (State, Defense and Justice) and agencies (CIA, DIA, and NSA). There were no international students this time due to the high security clearance needed to attend. In keeping with the theme of my entire military career, it was the classmates and the relationships developed (now at the senior level) that proved to be the most valuable aspect of the experience. [Out of that class, five or six of us went on to achieve four-star rank. One soldier, Hugh Shelton, achieved the highest military office when he became Chairman of the Joint Chiefs.]

The speakers who gave the lectures and made presentations were remarkable in that they represented the very best from their organizations, both in and out of government. Thanks to a strict non-attribution policy at the school, there was no reluctance to share the good, the bad and the ugly with us. It was a truly amazing time as combatant commanders, the chairman and service chiefs, members of Congress, Secretaries of Defense and State, agency heads, ambassadors, statesmen, historians and politicians in and out of government came to speak to us. The level of experience, expertise, and professionalism to which we were exposed was rare. Between the students in my class and the quality of the instructors and guest lecturers, it was a thrilling year.

As a lieutenant colonel, I was one of the junior officers at the college so it probably surprised many when I was selected to be a battalion commander at Camp Lejeune; surprising, because most of my classmates were already colonels and looking forward to command of a regiment, a group, a ship, or assignment to a high-level staff billet.

RUNNING THE MARINE CORPS MARATHON WHILE AT THE NATIONAL WAR COLLEGE

For me, the opportunity to command Marines was all that mattered. Yes, as a lieutenant colonel commanding a battalion, I would not put to use the operational and strategic instruction I received at the National War College, but the opportunity to rub elbows and share leadership challenges, with others, while at the college was invaluable and contributed to my overall professional growth. This interaction with them coupled with the quality of the instruction and the guest speakers assured me that it would not go to waste by my being a battalion commander. It would remain with me for use in future assignments. I advise professionals in the military or in civilian fields, don't turn down a chance to attend a course, and learn something from everyone you meet there.

Chapter 20

Battalion Command

"You must care more about the people you are privileged to lead than about yourself."

--General Al Gray, U.S. Marine Corps (Ret)

1983—1985

Camp Lejeune, North Carolina

After graduating from the National War College, I headed for Camp Lejeune and command. I had been chosen to take over 5th Battalion, 10th Marines (5/10), a self-propelled artillery battalion. I was very excited to have a field command again. We moved the family back to Camp Lejeune and rented an off-base house for a few months while waiting for on-base housing.

The turmoil I experienced back in the 70s was long gone facilitated by the end of a fractious war, the abolishment of the draft, and most importantly, the institution of the all-volunteer force. Now I found young men and women who wanted to be Marines and were for the most part high school graduates, better educated and truly motivated. Gone were the days of court ordered Marines or those who had police records. In this refreshing environment, the emphasis was on training, equipment maintenance and readiness. Though budget dollars were tight as they always are in peacetime, affecting training and readiness, it was an exciting time to be there.

Just as I assumed command, the Marine Corps decided to reorganize my battalion, and it was about to more than double in size. Instead of three batteries of 155 Howitzers and a headquarters battery, it was adding three batteries of 8-inch howitzers, bringing the total to six firing batteries, all self-propelled. At that time, it was the largest artillery battalion in the Marine Corps.

We were breaking new ground with such a large organization, and it was the perfect time to take over command. Considering the reorganized structure, we were a unique organization and had the luxury of figuring out how to do things on our own terms. I didn't inherit a set of issues which needed adjustment and didn't have to come in and fix things that had been done, or left undone, by someone before me.

It was an ideal situation; the decision to significantly enlarge the size of the battalion afforded me the opportunity to really shake up the entire battalion and get them energized in everything they did. The challenge was that each battery commander was different and had his own way of doing business. I focused their efforts by my commander's intent so they learned my expectations, but I left it up to them to figure out how to do it. To assist in making this happen, I assembled all of my officers and staff non-commissioned officers and talked to them about my expectations of them and what they could expect from me.

"My sense is there are many in the battalion that aren't happy being in a self-propelled outfit; that because we're too big, we'll never be deployed," I told them and for a moment I flashed back to Getlin's Corner, addressing my Marines that morning after the battle. A much different—more somber—tone to be sure, but also memorable moment of feeling that electric-thrill of addressing men under my command when the stakes were high. "There are some that feel all we'll ever do is maintain the equipment in the gunpark and never get to exercises." I swept the room pausing for a fraction of a second on each man. "Marines, we are going to move, shoot and communicate with the best of them. With your support and leadership, we are going to become the go to artillery outfit in the division. We may not deploy as a battalion, but each of the six firing batteries is going to be ready to deploy at a moment's notice, and we will prove to all that we are 'First Among Equals' when it comes to providing rapid, accurate fire support." I watched them for signs. "Any questions?" There were none as a group, but I knew individually there was much to discuss. "Okay, let's get started. Dismissed."

Immediately I started moving people around, fired up those who seemed to lack enthusiasm and began the process of getting folks engaged and excited about being in 5/10. We ran as a battalion in formation each Friday as a means to develop Esprit de Corps and to let the other units and organizations in the division know that, *Fifth is First!* I insisted that they go to the field for training and exercises as often as possible. The battalion went to Fort Bragg twice a year for training and live-fire shoots, and each battery was constantly firing from different locations throughout Camp Lejeune. We even had the base develop new firing positions for us to use. It was a busy, exciting time for the battalion.

From day one I intended to grow the feeling that it was a great place to work and my Marines made it happen! It was akin to the Fresh Air initiative of General Wilson, only, this time, I was the initiator. All of a sudden, people were glad to be a part of 5/10, and we developed an esprit that was the envy of those around us. I encouraged a friendly competition between my seven battery commanders and, in no time, their response was something to behold. No longer was the 5th Battalion the stepchild of the regiment.

Considering the new composition and size of the battalion, my staff and I had to learn on the job how to balance the training, manning, maintenance and logistics needs of each battery and the battalion. My staff welcomed the challenges, and after I provided commander's guidance and made sure they understood my intent, they ran with it. They would come back with thoughtful courses of action and recommendations and then I would make the decision. As we learned by doing, we made some mistakes, but on the whole, we quickly came up to speed. The schoolhouses had taught me well, and I insisted that we use the Marine Corps planning process in all we did.

In such a large organization, there were many demands on my time. Most of my days were spent not in my office but visiting the batteries, whether they were out in the field or in garrison. I was a very visible presence in and around the batteries and battalion area. My presence served two purposes—giving me a greater awareness of the command climate, and more importantly, letting them know that I was interested in them. Each one of the batteries had its own command and control organization that was responsible for the day to day function of the battery and the people comprising it. The battery commanders reported to me. They all knew me and, once again, I had the opportunity to observe, listen, inquire, question and mentor—everything involved in the day-to-day operations of each unit. Writing performance evaluations (we call them Fitness Reports) on these commanders was difficult because I had to rate them against each other, i.e. #1 of 7 captains, #2 of 7 and so forth. This was tough since they were all professionals and committed to excellence. I was fortunate to have great young leaders who were enthusiastic, energetic and professional in the way they led their batteries and cared for their people.

There was a lot of healthy competition between the six firing batteries and this helped foster their growth and development. I never expected we would deploy as a battalion, but I anticipated that individual batteries would deploy in support of infantry units. Accordingly, it was important that each unit was proficient, professional and prepared. This was my goal as the battalion commander and it naturally became the goal for each battery and served as the stimulus for the healthy competition. Each battery wanted to prove that they were the very best that they could be.

I use the phrase healthy competition to describe the absolutely intoxicating and enthusiastic command climate within the battalion, brought about by everyone striving toward the same goals. By contrast, I see unhealthy competition as people performing with only one thought in mind—to boost their reputation and their position within an organization. It was important for me to ensure that the folks leading the batteries under my command were acting as engaged leaders and getting the best out of their people, and not competing simply to boost their reputation or position within the battalion. To ensure that they kept things in proper perspective, I often reminded them of a phrase I had heard years before: '*There ain't no tree so tall that a small dog can't pee on it.*' It seemed to work!

That spirit of healthy competition was fun, as each battery wanted to outshine the others while making the battalion look terrific. As a leader, I encouraged it because I was convinced that the certain outcome of such competition was operational excellence and readiness. There was also vigorous rivalry between the other battalion commanders and me. The atmosphere was contagious, and I was blessed that my Marines, from private to sergeant major and from lieutenant to major, ensured that 5th was indeed first in all we did.

As my two-year tour as battalion commander regretfully came to an end, I was notified that I had been selected for colonel and assigned to Central Command, a combatant command located on MacDill Air Force Base in Tampa, Florida. It was a new opportunity for sure but a long way from command and my Marines. There was no doubt in my mind that I would now put my relationships, education and experience gleaned at the National War College to good use.

MY PROMOTION TO COL. AND CHANGE OF COMMAND CEREMONY WITH GOOD FRIEND LT. COL. JACK GLASGOW

Chapter 21

GOING JOINT | U.S. Central Command

"The only place success comes before work is in the dictionary." --Vince Lombardi

1985— 1988

MacDill Air Force Base

Tampa, Florida

Joint duty, ugh!

That was my first reaction to reading my new orders. I guess I wasn't really surprised with the assignment since it was a direct result of recent congressional legislation. In 1986, Congress passed the Goldwater-Nichols Act. In addition to establishing additional regional commands, it put into law the importance of joint duty assignments, in multiservice commands, for career officers. It mandated that one had to attend joint education courses and complete a joint assignment during their career. Congress was not satisfied that the military services were prepared for planning, training, operating, and if necessary, fighting in a joint manner. Historically, each service preferred to do their own thing, oftentimes not taking advantage of what one of the other services might bring to the effort. This requirement for joint education and assignments was particularly important for those individuals the services had earmarked for consideration for possible promotion to flag/general rank. In essence, the message Congress was sending to all services was, "No joint education and assignments, no promotion to general or admiral!"

Since I was finishing up a command slot, I was fair game and received orders assigning me to the U.S. Central Command located in Tampa, Florida. I was not happy about leaving the Marine Corps for a joint assignment and had some apprehension going to a command responsible for countries I had little to no knowledge of. At the same time, the opportunity to learn about this part of the world was exciting as was the chance to work with folks from the other services and government agencies.

We bought a house on the Gulf Coast, near the beach. This location made my commute to Tampa a lot longer, but we figured, what's the point of being in Florida if you're not going to live near the beach? Our house had a screened-in pool, which was exciting for the kids and eased the transition into a new neighborhood. As an added bonus, my sister Nancy and her family lived nearby, and her son A.J. and daughter Julie were the same ages as Andrew and Amy, giving the cousins their first opportunity to be together.

Once we got the kids settled in, I drove to U.S. Central Command (CENTCOM), which was about forty-five-minutes from home. I was now a colonel, assigned to the J-5 Directorate as Chief of the Policy/Strategy Division. My directorate boss was a one-star Navy rear admiral, and the CENTCOM commander at that time was Army General Bob Kingston. There were also three or four colonels from other services running other divisions within the J-5 Directorate.

It was a command with a smorgasbord of all services including Marines, soldiers, sailors, airmen and folks from the Coast Guard, as well as representatives from most of the governmental agencies to include the CIA, DOS, FBI, NSA, and DIA. This was a whole new environment for me, one that I wasn't initially very comfortable in.

My division was involved in the development and implementation of strategic plans and policies affecting the countries in CENTCOM's region of the world. I had no experience with the Middle East, so every day, early on, was a learning experience.

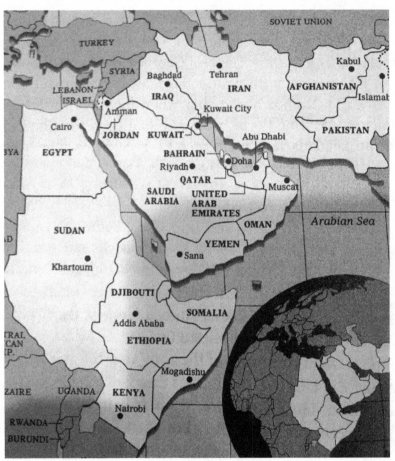

CENTCOM'S AREA OF RESPONSIBILITY

Once again, I found myself in a highly competitive environment and felt I was at a slight disadvantage. The other colonels had more joint staff experience than I did, simply because I had spent most of my time in the Marine Corps actually *in* the Marine Corps. They had spent a lot of time in their respective services, as well as having time at the Pentagon, in joint assignments. It was unusual for someone of my age and rank to have not yet been to the Pentagon. My only staff tour had been when I served as monitor and aide at Headquarters Marine Corps—a far cry from anything resembling a joint tour and that situation may have even been one of the reasons for the congressional legislation.

About a year after my arrival, General Kingston retired and was replaced by a Marine. General George Crist had a reputation as a tough taskmaster, both within the Marine Corps and the joint-services world. Rumor had it that when he was transferred from Headquarters Marine Corps, where he had been the Chief of Staff, people at headquarters celebrated. I received phone calls and messages from my 'friends' at Headquarters:

"Butch, my condolences, you're about to undergo a life-changing event with the arrival of General Crist!"

"Lucky you. Cancel all leave, change your running schedule, and forget about keeping your Florida tan, there's a new sheriff coming to town!"

"I hope you like staff work because you are about to meet the Man Who Loves Staff work!"

It turned out that their loss was our gain. General Crist was a true Agent of Change. He shook things up—and they were things that needed shaking up. This was a fairly new command, and it did not compare in importance to European Command or Pacific Command; accordingly, it was not the most desired of joint assignments unless one was getting ready to retire. Prior to his arrival, I sensed a complacency on the part of many of the folks there and the lack of a Can-Do attitude.

General Crist did not suffer fools gladly and, immediately upon his arrival, made it abundantly clear he expected nothing short of excellence from his staff officers. If he believed a senior officer (usually a colonel) was not measuring up, he would tell his boss to get rid of him, or at the very least, ensure that the officer never got in front of him again.

We quickly found that General Crist was a chain smoker. This made for some uncomfortable meetings with him, particularly when using the small conference room next to his office. I often brought documents in for his review and the room would be blue with cigarette smoke (I could barely see the table top and documents; it was so thick). It was pure torture for a non-smoker such as me to stay focused while he studied each sentence in detail.

During briefings, if the general asked someone a question they were supposed to know the answer to but didn't, he often ended the briefing at that moment. He would then meet with that individual's boss and, in many instances, the offending officer's briefing duties were terminated. Then, the officer was likely banished to the Mole Hole, an empty building in a remote part of MacDill where several colonels who failed to measure up to General Crist's demanding standards had the dubious distinction of being condemned pending reassignment or retirement.

YOU'RE NAÏVE, NEAL

My division was responsible for reviewing most of the Pentagon documents affecting strategy and policy for our region of the world. One day, I was asked to brief the general on a newly received document that related to joint forces assigned to different commands around the world. General Crist was very familiar with this document from his previous post at the Pentagon; it wouldn't be stretching it to say he was practically its author.

We had previously gone over it with him, and he had made clear what he wanted to be modified or removed from it. My task was to brief him and his senior staff on the outcome of our scrub of the document and our dialogue with the Joint Staff. I did not realize that

I was about to experience another *What Now, Lieutenant?* moment during the briefing.

When I arrived for the briefing, all the principals on the staff—generals and admirals—were sitting around the table.

I said, "I know, General, that you don't like this one paragraph in the document. I've gone back to the Joint Staff with your changes. They understood your concerns and told me they would incorporate your changes with the next addendum or rewrite of the document."

He immediately yelled, "Stop! That's the problem with you, Neal! You're a field Marine and have never had a real staff assignment, and you're naïve when it comes to understanding this document and how the Joint Staff works!"

My Irish temper took immediate hold as I quickly responded, "I may be naïve sir, but in this particular case, I don't think I am wrong."

The silence was deafening. My directorate boss, the admiral, was doing what we all routinely called 'the bent shoe routine.' Whenever things got hot with the general, all the principals seemed to find a problem with their shoes, thus avoiding eye contact with General Crist. For a long, seemingly endless, moment General Crist locked on me as he inhaled on his ever-present cigarette and then barked, "Continue!"

I finished my part of the briefing and was dismissed. As I left the conference room, I was acutely aware of what everyone in that briefing room was thinking: "Neal's going to the Mole Hole!" I thought so too, as I returned to my office. Minutes later, after the general left the briefing room, my boss, the admiral came running into my office. Red faced, with perspiration running off his brow, he sputtered to me, "Butch! What were you doing in there?" He worried that we both might be headed in the same direction.

"Sir, I was completely confident in what I just said. That's why I said it. They will change it, but not until the rewrite."

I did not get sent to the Mole Hole and, sure enough, very shortly thereafter, the rewrite came out and the change I described had indeed been included. General Crist never said a word to me about that but, thereafter, whenever I made a comment or briefed him, he took me at my word. I had won his confidence by standing up to him, and it was a seminal moment. I was pissed that he'd called me naïve and doubted my comments. By pushing back, I had demonstrated I possessed the courage of my convictions and made it clear that I was not one to back down if I thought I was right.

Obviously, he liked what he saw that day. As an unintended consequence, I became one of General Crist's trusted agents and a go-to scribe in terms of dealing with policy issues and writing messages and papers under his name.

[This is a good teaching point: Don't back down if you feel like you're right—and don't let yourself be intimidated! This is difficult to impress upon young folks—particularly when they are confronting seniors with greater knowledge and experience. I understand being disinclined to push back with senior officers—or authority—when you are not comfortable or confident in your position. But, if you have done your homework and you're well prepared and you know you're right, there should be no need to step back. After all, leaders want and expect from their staffs solid, well-reasoned answers to their questions. Even when they're ones they don't expect and may not particularly like at the time.]

LEARNING TO SAY, "I DON'T KNOW"

[Something else to keep in mind along this same line is not being afraid to say "I don't know." This is tough for anyone to say, particularly when it is your responsibility to know. The experience, and its memory, that solidified this for me was when I was a brand new major working in Manpower Management at headquarters. A Colonel Marty Julian had asked me a question I should have known the answer to; I didn't, but I attempted to give him some bullshit response. He knew I was scrambling for some semblance of an answer, and he literally ripped me a new rear end. From that moment on, I swore that I would never again shoot from the hip when queried and would not be afraid to say "I don't know." This lesson learned helped me later in my career.]

Another incident involving General Crist also contains an important teaching point. One Saturday, I had written a message for the general and waited for his review of it. I wasn't the first, and I wouldn't be the last to be kept waiting by him. He was notorious for keeping senior officers stewing in the hallway while he pored, word by word, over whatever message you'd written for him. I became frustrated and wanted to go home. Since I had recently written so many messages for the general, I was comfortable that I had written it the way he wanted it, capturing all the salient points. I was tired of waiting and told General Crist's senior aide that my son had a wrestling meet I wanted to attend, and I was going home. And that's what I did.

No sooner had I walked through the front door than the phone rang. Kathy answered it and then looked at me and said, "It's the aide to General Crist, and apparently, the general wants to see the officer who wrote the message."

General Crist knew perfectly well that I was the one who had written it. So, I got on the phone with the aide and said, "Look, he knows I'm the one who wrote the message. Is there something wrong with it?"

The aide said, "No, he just said he wants to *see* the officer who wrote it!"

136

It's important to note that this was a Saturday morning, and this message was not related to any sort of urgent situation. The truth is, General Crist liked staff work and had no problem working twenty hours a day, seven days a week. Unfortunately, as I had been warned by those at headquarters, he was so dedicated to the job that he often forgot the impact that his work habits had on his personnel. He didn't take into consideration that others might have a life outside of work in the Marine Corps and a desire to spend weekend time at home, with their families, whenever possible. Had we been at war, with missiles coming at us, that twenty-four/seven approach to work would have been one thing, but a message written on a Saturday morning during peacetime certainly could have waited until Monday morning.

I reluctantly got in my car and drove through weekend traffic back to MacDill. When I got there, the aide said, "The general says the message is fine. You can go now."

General Crist was reminding me who was the boss and letting me know that he was the one who would tell me when I could and could not leave. It was a lesson learned. Our relationship had grown after the briefing incident, and I had felt like the general's golden boy—so much so that it may have gone to my head a little bit and caused me to overstep my bounds. My unilateral decision to inform the general's aide that I was heading home caused the general to see the need to put me back in my place. And to remind me that, when he said he wanted you to wait while he looked over a message you'd written on his behalf, you were expected to wait. In spite of that incident, and the fact that General Crist had traits that didn't meet my leadership metrics, I had high regard for him, learned much from him, and we enjoyed a good relationship.

THE MIDDLE EAST

During my time at CENTCOM, a series of events led to me spending the better part of two years in the Middle East, assisting several countries in learning the military planning process. We had discovered that many of the countries in our area of responsibility (AOR) did not have a good understanding of military planning procedures and we determined, rightly so, that it was to our advantage to aid and assist them in learning and using this process within their respective militaries.

General Crist worked with the Pentagon to establish a very sensitive planning team under the direction of the CENTCOM Inspector General, Marine Brigadier General Jed Pierson. I was designated as the team leader.

In advance of spending time in the Middle East, we took the time to study the culture of each country we were tasked with training. We all read books and papers in preparation for our travels to help us to be sensitive to the cultural differences and traditions found in both the region and in the individual countries we would be working with. Reading to prepare myself was great but a massive amount of learning came simply by doing. Nothing could have substituted for being there in person and learning as we went along, much like my experience as an advisor in Vietnam. We flew back and forth between MacDill and the Middle East on a routine basis. The team would go to the Middle East for fifteen days or so and then return and report on our progress to General Crist and folks at the Pentagon. There was no predetermined time for us to make a return trip but word got out in the AOR, and we began to receive more requests for the team.

Despite the absences from home, it was a great couple of years. It gave me an opportunity to assist in the building of military-to-military relationships with the future leaders of various Middle East countries.

[Little did we know at the time that these relationships and training would pay such great dividends later on. At the time, we weren't anticipating going to war together but later, during Desert Shield and Desert Storm when General Schwarzkopf (who in 1990 replaced the retiring General Crist at CENTCOM) and our nation formed a coalition in partnership with various countries against Iraq, I would walk into the Coalition Command Center and be amazed to see many of the very same men. We knew them, and they knew us, and it was our good fortune to work alongside these men we had trained and worked with two years prior. Having those relationships already established allowed us to understand each other from the get-go without having to get up to speed. They were already intimately familiar with the U.S. planning procedures, which were what the coalition used.]

Once again, one of the gifts and lessons from this tour was the reinforcement of the importance of relationships in our profession. But this tour had taken that to a whole different level, as I had to learn to develop relationships with folks in other countries—folks with customs, beliefs and habits entirely foreign to my own. I had to learn to deal with them, engage with them, and gain their trust while, at the same time, both meeting and managing their expectations.

I finished up my time in the Middle East with a better appreciation that while we may be very different people, in the most fundamental ways, we are all the same. For the most part, we all share the same desires, goals, and aspirations. Our worldviews may differ based on where we sit but most people love their families, have some sort of faith, and basically want to live in peace.

New orders arrived, so we sold the house, packed up the car and drove back to Quantico. I would be taking over as Director of Amphibious Warfare School. To tell you the truth, we hated leaving

Florida. Just as in every assignment, it was difficult leaving the new friends we had made and the great home we lived in. At the same time, we looked forward to reconnecting with our many old friends in the Quantico area.

CHAPTER 22

AMPHIBIOUS WARFARE SCHOOL (DIRECTOR)

"The direction in which education starts a man will determine his future life." --Plato

1988—1990

QUANTICO, VIRGINIA

We moved into the house at Quantico designated for the director of the school. Our son Andrew was starting his sophomore year at college by now, and our daughters Erin and Amy were, respectively, a freshman and junior in high school. No move was ever easy but having a house on base meant that we didn't have to search for one, and that made the move as easy as it could have been.

Having attended and taught at AWS, I was very familiar with the school and knew most of the civilian staff that provided the continuity there. This made for an easy transition for me, and I felt fortunate being back in familiar territory. All of the instructors were top-of-the-line majors and lieutenant colonels. They were enthusiastic, well qualified professionals, steeped in experience, and just the kind of teacher-leaders you wanted instructing young captains. I felt blessed to be in charge of them.

It was a two-year assignment and both years were just wonderful. General Gray [whom you may recall from his debriefing of me after the Battle of Getlin's Corner back when he was a major] had become Commandant of the Marine Corps. Committed to reinvigorating the professional development and education of his

Marines, he was very interested in the principles of maneuver warfare. He had studied and embraced the writings of civilian academic Bill Lind and retired Air Force Colonel John Boyd. [I would have both as guest lecturers at AWS several times while I served as director.] Their writings combined with the force of personality and commitment of General Gray to introduce maneuver warfare into the school's curriculum were critically important. I was fortunate to have a close personal and professional friend nearby, Colonel Paul Van Riper, assigned as the Director of the Command and Staff College; we were both maneuver warfare advocates. General Gray probably stacked the deck, selecting Van Riper and me specifically for the purpose of introducing it into the schoolhouses.

The students quickly picked up on it and embraced its precepts. You could feel their enthusiasm, both in the classroom and during exercises. They realized and accepted that it was important to convey commander's intent and what needed to be accomplished and trust your subordinates to figure out the 'How.' We were teaching these young captains not only to think but to do so differently. The classroom instruction was supplemented by a series of warfighting pamphlets commissioned and blessed by General Gray, and they contributed significantly to the true professional development of all Marines.

What Now, Lieutenant? questions were now being asked and applied at the captain level. For example:

"Given the mission statement and your analysis of it, how detailed should your commander's intent be?"

"How do you incorporate the writings of Lind and Boyd into your thought process and those of your subordinate leaders?"

"When will you be comfortable that your junior leaders fully understand your Commander's Intent and will develop their own 'How' in carrying out their mission?"

"How do you develop, educate, train and encourage trust tactics in your subordinates?"

When many of these captains left AWS, they would go on to become company commanders at places like Camp Lejeune and Camp Pendleton. Our challenge and commitment were to get them so well versed in maneuver warfare, commanders intent, and trust tactics that these things would become second nature in all they did. We were developing leaders who were doctrinally sound but not doctrinally bound. We were confident that, if they knew and understood the commander's intent, they could adjust as circumstances dictated, keep accomplishment of the mission uppermost in mind, and when necessary, call an audible.

There were two hundred or more captains at AWS, and at least 75 percent of those were married, which led to a lively social environment. There were many events planned as part of the school year, and my wife Kathy was heavily involved in them and hosted many functions at our house. The students' wives enjoyed the opportunity to get to know each other better and to share experiences.

Unfortunately, in the middle of our first year at AWS, Kathy was diagnosed with stage-three breast cancer with significant lymph node involvement. She was in her mid-forties and had a terrible family history with the disease. She underwent surgery, chemotherapy, and radiation. It was a serious time for our family, and it continued through the second year at AWS. The other wives were supportive and marveled over Kathy's resilience and her ability to continue with nearly all the activities she had been engaged with prior to her diagnosis. Not only was Kathy their mentor, but she also became their role model.

THE FIRST STAR

During the Christmas break of 1989, we traveled to Kathy's family house in South Boston for the holidays. We had made a conscious effort right from the start of our time in the Marine Corps to spend any time off in the Boston/Hull area to keep the kids connected with our families and their cousins. During this visit, we had gone out for a party, and when we returned, I had a message, "A General Gray called while you were out, wanting to talk to you, and asked you to give him a call back."

I knew that the Brigadier General's Selection Board had met in October and that I was in the zone under consideration. Without a doubt, selection for brigadier general was a tough process given all the highly-qualified officers and the likelihood of making the cut was less than ten percent. The question that immediately came to mind was whether General Gray was calling with good news or calling to console me.

With great trepidation, I returned his call. His first words upon answering were, "Welcome to the NFL!" By using that analogy, he was saying, "You're in the big leagues now!" Over the years, from Getlin's Corner to being a battalion commander in his division, to leading AWS for him, we had become and remained close, and he was clearly very happy and excited for me.

This was great news, and everyone was obviously very excited. I was now a Brigadier General Select. I finished out the year and received my orders to Headquarters Marine Corps in Washington, D.C. In anticipation of this new assignment, we bought a house in Northern Virginia and began moving in.

There was a promotion ceremony at Headquarters Marine Corps, officiated by General Gray. I invited all our relatives and many close friends, including John Prickett. John had recovered from his Vietnam injuries, had undergone a hip replacement, and was in pretty good shape. To look at him walking down the street, you wouldn't guess at the terrible ordeal he had survived. It took John some time to find the right girl to marry so he was a bit late in starting a family. In fact, he had to rush back after the ceremony to be with his wife, Lisa for the birth of their third daughter! Another special guest was General Sam Jaskilka, the former Assistant Commandant I had served under as an Aide.

PROMOTION TO BRIGADIER GENERAL WITH GENERALS GRAY AND JASKILKA

When General Gray spoke at the ceremony, he talked about how we had met in April of 1967 when he was a major and I was a lieutenant and had asked me those penetrating questions related to the Battle of Getlin's Corner. Then he moved forward in the chronology and covered my background, including the assignments I'd had and the awards I had received. "I'm delighted with your performance at the Amphibious Warfare School. You're a great warrior, educator, and trainer. You were selected and now promoted because you have much more to contribute to the Marine Corps."

He pinned one star on the collar of my shirt and one on my shoulder—the insignia representing my new rank. Then he invited Kathy up to do the same on the other collar, telling her not to worry whether or not she did it correctly because I would surely spend a lot of time in front of a mirror, making sure it was perfect.

CHAPTER 23

WHEN THE STORM BROKE

"The best thing you can do is the right thing; the next best thing you can do is the wrong thing; the worst thing you can do is nothing." --Theodore Roosevelt

1990—1992
DIRECTOR, MANPOWER PLANS AND POLICY DIVISION
WASHINGTON, D.C.

In my new assignment, I was to be stationed at Headquarters Marine Corps. It was going to be a very challenging job, as my team was charged with figuring out what manpower was needed to meet the requirements of the Marine Corps. But fate had plans of her own.

I reported to my new duty and was quickly getting up to speed. Less than a month into it, Kathy and I were traveling when we heard some startling news: Kuwait, my old stomping grounds, had been invaded by Saddam Hussein!

"Do you think you'll be involved?" she asked.

"No," I said. "With this new assignment, I'm sure I won't be going anywhere. This job is too important." But I didn't exactly relish the idea of being stuck in Washington D.C. if there was going to be a war in the Middle East. I needn't have worried about that as my twenty years between wars were about to end.

THE STORM

Several days later, the answer to Kathy's question was answered, and my opinion proved wrong. General Gray called and said, "Butch, Chairman Powell and the Joint Chiefs of Staff have asked that the Army and Marine Corps nominate a one-star to serve as Deputy for Operations for General Schwarzkopf in Saudi Arabia, someone with ground combat experience. Of course, I want to nominate you for this position," he explained. "With your ground combat experience—coupled with those special missions to the Middle East—you're ideal for the slot." He paused. "But I also want to be sensitive to what Kathy is going through so I figured I'd better check with you first. Do you think you can leave?"

"She's finished most of her treatment and is getting her strength back," I said. "Let me check with her and I'll get back to you, sir."

When I got home that evening, I was a bit tentative about talking to Kathy about it. We had just moved into a new house and were not yet settled. Both Amy and Erin were going through big changes; Amy was about to leave for her first year of college, and Erin was moving from a very small Quantico high school to one with more than a thousand students. Of course, my real concern about leaving was Kathy's medical condition and the debilitating effects of her treatment. Leaving her to deal with all of this by herself didn't seem fair. But Kathy, if you have not realized by now, is one tough cookie. She had to be, considering she grew up with six brothers and all the years of experience being the wife of a career Marine. As I asked her, I flashed back to when I had proposed to her so long ago—that yearning for the answer I wanted—but this was a far different circumstance. No matter what she decided, I would accept it.

"How could you not go?" she said. "You probably have more experience in that area of the world than most, and you know everything about the command."

"Yes, but I don't know General Schwartzkopf, and I'm sure all of the staff have turned over. I just know the last thing they will want to see is a brand-new BG showing up to 'save the day' for them."

"I'll worry about you. But you should go. Everything will be fine here."

I studied Kathy's face seeing the emotion in her eyes and realized again how special she truly was (and is). Her thoughts were about what was best for me and my career.

A couple of days later, she and Erin drove me to Dover Air Force Base where a plane waited to take me to Saudi Arabia. I was going to war again, only this time for the duration, and it was anyone's guess how long that would be. As we said our goodbyes, we didn't know when we would see each other again.

There was not any crowd of well-wishers awaiting me; no one was there to say goodbye to me except my family. As I boarded the C-5 (the biggest military transport plane in the U.S.) the young pilot told me, "General, I thought I should let you know you're the only passenger besides the crew because we're carrying hazardous cargo, we're loaded with ordinance."

Just what you want to hear—that you're on a plane full of ammunition! I took my seat in the section behind the pilot, the only passenger seated in the seventy-something seats. As we took off, I thought about the reality that I hadn't the faintest idea how long I would be gone. That went with the territory. I also had no idea who was on General Schwarzkopf's staff and had never met the general. I expected that staff had changed in the two years since I had been at CENTCOM. I was flying into the unknown, entering a war zone and, in military slang, being 'beamed in' to a new outfit. When you're beamed in, a chilly reception can await you from those who perceive your sudden appearance as a signal from the powers that be that the folks who are already on site are not up to the tasks at hand. You never know whether you will be received with open arms or resentment. All of this weighed heavily on my mind but did little to make the flight go faster.

Landing first in Germany, the fog was so thick that the follow-me truck sent to guide us into our parking space couldn't even find us. We switched crews and then continued on to Saudi. We landed in Dhahran, on the coast in humid weather, and then I caught another plane into Riyadh, the capital of Saudi Arabia. Having spent quite a bit of time there in those previous years, I pretty much knew my way around. The place was a beehive of activity and, everywhere I turned, there were troops, planes, and equipment moving in different directions. It was a chaotic environment as everyone and everything was flowing into Saudi in preparation for a possible war. Again, I flashed back to when I had headed into another war and stepped off that C-130 in Vietnam. Little did I know at the time what my two tours of duty would teach me and how much the death of my Brother Marines had affected me. I wondered what would come from this tour, in a region on the verge of war, where men and women could die or be wounded.

The following morning, I reported to General Schwarzkopf.

WORKING FOR GENERAL SCHWARZKOPF

RIYADH, SAUDI ARABIA

When I entered General Schwarzkopf's office, he was seated at his desk writing. I noticed he was left handed. He looked up at me expectantly.

"Sir, Brigadier General Neal reporting as ordered."

He looked me over, stood and greeted me with a warm, welcoming smile. I was struck first by his remarkable stature. At six-foot-three, as contrasted to my five-foot-six, he was a big man and towered over me. He was thick-chested, and it was obvious why his friends called him The Bear. A bit rounded in the shoulders he had huge forearms and, on each wrist, he wore a watch with the one on his right facing down.

"Welcome to CENTCOM and to Saudi Arabia. I feel as if I know you since Al Gray keeps calling to tell me how good you are. Hell, I know that. I've most of your record right here." He gestured at a file folder on his desk. "You've spent a lot of time in the region and know many of the officers from the countries in the coalition. That'll be helpful." I could tell he had read deep into my file when he asked me, "How did you like working with the Vietnamese as an advisor?"

"Sir, it was a terrific tour. The South Vietnamese Marines didn't need to be motivated—they were fighting to save their country. The leaders I worked with were true professionals. Except for having a wife and new son at home I would have liked to have stayed there with them to finish the job. They would've fought on, but they needed our logistics and air support. I feel we somehow let them down when we left."

He sat back down behind his desk. "Damn Butch, that's exactly how I felt when I finished my tour and had to leave. I asked to be extended, but the Army wouldn't hear of it." He then turned to the business at hand. "I need someone with ground combat experience in the J-3 Division. This is going to be a ground-centric fight and, as good as our aircraft and pilots are, it will take soldiers and Marines on the ground to drive the Iraqis out of Kuwait and reestablish its borders." He picked up my folder. "That means a tough infantry, armor, and artillery fight and I want to make sure I've someone in the J-3 shop that knows what ground combat is all about." He put the folder down and his eyes locked on mine. "That's you!"

At that moment, I could feel beads of sweat running down my back as he seemed to be making me bigger and better than I thought I was. Was this another *What Now, Lieutenant?* moment? "Sir, the one thing you can depend on is that I'll give you my full effort for as long as it takes. I will not hesitate to give you my best professional advice even if it's contrary to what you've decided to do."

No matter if he perceived what I'd just said rightly or wrongly, I wanted to set the expectation from the very beginning. Rumor had it that he had an easy to spark temper, and I was ready for what might come next. He stood up, all six million feet of him (at that moment he seemed that tall), came around and put his arm around my shoulder and said, "That's why you're here, Butch. I need someone to tell me when I might be showing my underwear."

From that moment on, I liked him and knew this was going to be a professionally challenging, yet rewarding, tour. As time went by, we would develop a strong personal relationship, as well.

General Schwarzkopf introduced me to everyone, including my new boss, Major General Burt Moore, an Air Force pilot who had joined the staff after a successful tour as the Director of Legislative Liaison Office for the Secretary of the Air Force. Tall, good looking with distinguished-looking gray hair that I swear the Air Force issues to all of their generals, I could tell from the outset that he was probably much more comfortable working in the Halls of Congress and the Pentagon than in an underground bunker in Saudi Arabia. Just as obvious, I could tell that he and General Schwarzkopf were not particularly close. And Moore was clearly not happy to see me. I suspect he viewed me with suspicion and was no doubt concerned I might be there to replace him—an eventuality that was highly unlikely and the furthest thing from my mind.

The first thing General Schwarzkopf wanted me to do before joining the J-3 division was to walk around and get a sense of the command and give him any changes I might recommend for improving the staff's ability to assist him in making warfighting decisions. He was looking for a fresh set of eyes on how the command was organized and working as it moved closer and closer to possible offensive operations. I wasn't entirely comfortable poking my nose into everyone's business and asking questions, as I felt it might engender further distrust of me since I was an outsider to begin with.

Nevertheless, I did as he requested and was surprised to find that many on the staff were doing things as if they were still in Florida rather than in Saudi Arabia preparing for war. From my perspective, they were operating with a business as usual mindset, at half speed, with no particular sense of urgency. They hadn't embraced the fact that there was a strong possibility we were going to war.

Given the general's notorious temper, I was cautious in reporting this to him and couched my observations accordingly: "My sense is that a lot of people here never expected to be deployed." His look at me was penetrating as I continued, "and they are operating as if they are still *in* Tampa. The practices, procedures, and meetings used there are still in effect here." I looked him in the eye and saw the lines settle and deepen on his face. I took a deep breath; I had to shoot straight with him without any sugar-coating on it. "Frankly, sir, I'm concerned that they aren't prepared to provide you with the wherewithal to make warfighting decisions."

"At last" he bellowed, "someone has the same impression I have. A lot of folks just don't get it; they don't grasp the fact that we're almost surely going to war!"

I was relieved to hear that and fortunately, General Schwarzkopf's Chief of Staff, Major General Bob Johnson, had the same concerns. Like me, he was worried that the staff was not geared, organized and focused toward providing General Schwarzkopf with the information he needed to make good decisions. He was already working to flesh out the staff, augmenting it with personnel possessing skill sets they didn't currently have on the team. At the same time, he was firing up the staff and its leadership to drive the message into them; they were a long way from Tampa, and it was time they put on their warfighting faces. It was common knowledge that many of them had sought positions in Tampa because they saw it as a great place to prepare for retirement. Now, all of a sudden, these folks who'd thought they made a great move found themselves in a war zone. This cocoon of complacency was a weakness that General Schwarzkopf had already noted, and I confirmed by virtue of my walk-through. But things were going to change, and quickly.

THE JEDI KNIGHTS

There were a lot of folks being beamed in as this was the 'only war in town.' The J-3 staff was a good one, run by a sharp Marine colonel named Tony Gain. He was General Moore's go to man, and he was nervous that I would be moving him out of his job. Nothing could be further from the truth. I learned a long time ago that if you have a fast horse, ride him, and Tony was just that. He was superb, and we worked well as a team. Getting to know the command staff was pretty easy; they were all good folks, and most knew why I was there and welcomed me.

Those that probably had the most difficult time being accepted by the staff were military planners who were brought in, at General Schwarzkopf's direction, to do the operations planning for the ground offensive. Just think of it, you had an entire J-5 Directorate run by a Navy admiral with the talent and responsibility for such planning being sidelined by the introduction of Lt. Col. Joe Purvis and three other Army officers. These planners were immediately sequestered in their own room and for all intent and purposes worked directly for General Schwarzkopf.

Known as the Special Plans Group, these four officers representing Army armor, logistics and infantry expertise were tasked by the general to develop a plan that made the most of the forces assigned should the decision be made to forcefully drive Iraqi forces out of Kuwait. There was no Marine Corps planner in the group. That and the fact that they were beamed in, secretive in nature and virtually isolated from the rest of the staff, led to them being labeled the Jedi Knights. That was not a term of endearment as far as the J-5 planners were concerned.

You can imagine how their presence impacted the morale of those on the staff whose job it was to do such planning; it was thoroughly demoralizing. The problem was they didn't have all the answers, and without taking advantage of the expertise resident in the CENTCOM planning staff, the product the Knights would eventually come up with—an Army-centric concept of operations— failed to consider all the forces available or required.

It was in this atmosphere that I reported to General Moore as his deputy for operations. From the first moment, I met him it was clear he thought I was moving in on his territory. I particularly remember one of the first staff meetings I attended. He acted as if I wasn't even there and basically cut me out of the discussion. I was not invited to make recommendations, and he was not receptive to my ideas. He had his own team of very good people, but there were certain areas where I was sure my experience and expertise would be of value. It was during that meeting General Moore tasked someone other than me with checking out a particular issue that the commander had asked about.

I spoke up and said, "I'll take care of that sir since I'm already working on it."

"No," he said, "I want *him* to do this!"

I turned to everyone in the room and said, "Hey folks, I need to talk to the boss. I need everyone to leave us alone for a while." It was a come-to-Jesus moment, maybe even a *What Now, Lieutenant?* moment. When the room cleared, I said, "Look, if you don't want me here, that's fine. I have no problem asking to be reassigned to the Marine Corps, but, I remind you, the general wants me here."

He looked at me and said, "Are you threatening me?"

"No," I said, "I'm just telling you the facts. I cannot operate in a situation like this, where I'm not trusted or treated as due my rank and position. Believe me, I'm here to help you do your job, not make myself look important."

After that, we got along fairly well. I don't know whether he ever really accepted my presence there, but he slowly and begrudgingly started to allow me to have input in situations where my background and expertise enabled me to really be of help. Over time, I felt that General Schwarzkopf never really gave General Moore his due or recognized his excellence, and that made him insecure. The truth is, he had a lot of good points and a lot to offer to the staff and the command. But that was one of General Schwarzkopf's failings. If you somehow managed to get on his bad side, there was no way to correct that and very little chance of redemption. Whatever the source of friction between him and General Schwarzkopf, General Moore couldn't overcome it. And this was unfortunate because I felt he was never really given a chance.

CHAPTER 24

DESERT SHIELD: A BUILD-UP FOR WAR

"The skillful general conducts his army as if he were leading a single man by the hand." --Sun Tzu

2 AUGUST 1990 – 17 JANUARY 1991

RIYADH, SAUDI ARABIA

From September until January, we were engaged in four critical tasks: deploying forces to the theater, planning for offensive operations to eject the Iraqis out of Kuwait, building a coalition of nation states that could provide forces to aid and assist us in this effort, and developing the logistics sustainment base for executing the mission at hand. We had to build up huge quantities of fuel, ammunition, food, water and accoutrements for conducting an operation against the enemy. Of course, this was connected to the deployment of all forces from Europe and the U.S. and the deployment of coalition forces. Many of the coalition forces did not have self-deploying capability and needed our assistance with getting to Saudi Arabia.

It was a mammoth undertaking, deploying our U.S. forces to the area while at the same time assisting in the deployment of European and coalition forces. No other nation could have done what our folks did in making it happen. Those four efforts were the primary tasks we worked on day in and day out. While they were the focus during Desert Shield, the command continued to ensure that Iraqi forces did not attempt any encroachment into Saudi Arabia.

The Saudis had built mini-cities for the nomadic Bedouin tribes that wandered and lived in the Saudi desert, but the Bedouins did not want to give up their tents or their way of life. And over the years, the Saudis had invested vast amounts of money on military infrastructure for the defense of the Kingdom. Command centers, reinforced buildings, and aircraft hangars are only a few examples of the excess and empty infrastructure available for use by incoming coalition forces. All around the city of Riyadh, there were buildings ready for occupation. The vacant facilities were ideal for housing a significant number of our troops.

CENTCOM had moved into an enormous state-of-the-art underground command center in central Riyadh. It was wired, air conditioned and large enough to accommodate both the staff and the coalition headquarters people. There were two distinct command centers, one for the U.S. and one for the coalition, but they were within walking distance of each other in the same underground building. They afforded us almost a plug-and-play capability and made the transition from Tampa that much easier. This is not to say that being stuck in a command center in Riyadh was without its challenges, but it was a whole lot better than tents in the desert.

Our previous training paid big dividends during Desert Shield/Desert Storm. A good portion of the countries that came together in the coalition against Iraqi forces had been trained by us during our previous mission in the Middle East. Trying to do that kind of training *in extremis,* on the fly, would have put us at a disadvantage.

General Schwarzkopf wanted to initiate the fight on his own timeline—setting the conditions for success to his satisfaction—and he was disinclined to conduct any offensive action against Iraqi forces before he felt we were ready, although many opportunities to do so presented themselves. He wanted to have in place all of the military forces required and the logistics necessary to sustain them before he gave the order to attack. These are only a few examples of the conditions he imposed on the force before he, and he alone, would give the order to start both the air campaign and subsequently the ground offensive:

"What preliminary actions are required before we are prepared to initiate the air campaign?"

"No incursions into Iraq or Kuwait by our forces until I say so, and I mean No!"

"What kind of deception operations can we execute to confuse the enemy?"

"I want the Republican Guard tanks (considered to be the elite Iraqi fighting force) reduced 50 percent by our aircraft before we cross the line of departure (LOD)."

"Damn it, I need better collection capabilities so I know when the conditions I've set for initiating ground combat are met!"

I clearly recall a discussion about boots where General Schwarzkopf became irate over the slow delivery of desert combat boots, to the point of throwing one across the table at the J-4, Major General Dane Stallings.

"Damn it, I want these boots, and I want them now" be bellowed as the boot flew by General Stallings' ear.

"Yes sir, I understand, and I'm confident they're on the way."

"You better be more than confident; you better be right! Understand?"

This was not the only incident, of this type, that occurred. It happened on enough occasions that I worried for the survival of some of the key leadership staff. This was a notable shortcoming of General

Schwarzkopf, his tendency to lose his temper and chew out senior officers in an open forum with subordinates present. Such actions are contrary to good leadership and a flaw that the general had a tough time containing. But it's no surprise that General Schwarzkopf was stressed on many levels. After all, he had politicians, senior military, and coalition members to deal with while at the same time trying to prepare for war. There were plenty of things to peg out his stress meter!

Of critical importance to the success of the effort was the fact that Chairman Powell knew how to handle General Schwarzkopf to the benefit of all. Because they were lifelong friends from the Army and enjoyed a great professional and personal relationship, Chairman Powell always knew how to recognize when General Schwarzkopf was getting fired up or on the verge of losing his temper, and more importantly, how to calm him down. When it became obvious that General Schwarzkopf was putting too much pressure on his staff—because his temper was flaring—Chairman Powell prudently told him, "Norm, you need a deputy for something this big, so I am sending you Cal Waller to help you run the command."

Chairman Powell wisely identified the need for a buffer between General Schwarzkopf and the staff. Lieutenant General Waller had worked for or with General Schwarzkopf no less than seven times and knew him inside and out. On the general's side, he liked General Waller and depended on and confided in him. It was a relationship made in Heaven. Sure enough, when General Waller showed up, and General Schwarzkopf went off on a tirade and started yelling and screaming, General Waller would say, "Okay, Sir, I know exactly what you want. Calm down. I got it." Once General Schwarzkopf left the war room, General Waller would say, "Anyone know what he was so excited about and, more importantly, how we can fix it?"

He was perfect for the command and, more importantly, for the staff. He saved the day and probably a lot of careers. He might have even saved a couple of the junior generals from jumping off tall buildings.

THE PLAN

In October, General Schwarzkopf dispatched Major General Bob Johnson, his Chief of Staff, and his planning team to Washington to brief Secretary of Defense Dick Cheney, Chairman Powell, the Joint Chiefs and ultimately the president on the air campaign and ground scheme of maneuver for kicking Iraq out of Kuwait. General Schwarzkopf was not particularly happy with the plan as written, believing he needed at least another corps (more men) to give him greater flexibility.

Brigadier General Buster Glosson briefed the air campaign, and you had to know Buster to appreciate him. Here again was a general with the Air Force issued gray hair, good looks and the bravado of a fighter pilot. He was something to behold when giving a briefing since in his mind there was absolutely nothing the Air Force couldn't accomplish without anyone having to dirty their boots. All you had to do is ask him, and he would confirm as much. To listen to him, you had to question why we were even deploying ground forces to the fight. General Glosson's presentation was smooth and basically guaranteed success.

Colonel Joe Purvis of the Jedi Knights briefed the ground campaign which was for all intent and purposes a conventional high-diddle-diddle-up-the-middle approach. To say that it was not well received would be an understatement. The ground plan failed to impress either Secretary Cheney or Chairman Powell. Because the air campaign was so attractive, they were concerned that once President Bush heard both briefs, he might be inclined to go with just the air campaign, scratching the ground campaign altogether. Realistically, who could blame him!

The next stop was the White House to brief President Bush and his top officials. Generals Powell and Schwarzkopf instructed General Glosson to tone down his briefing which was like telling a politician to stop talking. As expected, even dialed down it was still well received by all while, predictably, the ground campaign briefing was unanimously declared to be 'awful!' This is where Chairman Powell jumped in:

"Mr. President we don't want you to come away with the idea that an air campaign alone could achieve your objective of removing Iraqi forces from Kuwait." He emphasized, "it will take the combined efforts of air, ground and coalition forces to accomplish the mission you've set out." General Powell won the day, avoiding an air only campaign and was even authorized an additional corps to augment the ground forces.

When General Johnson returned to Saudi, he sat down with General Schwarzkopf and in great detail debriefed him on what had transpired in Washington. Afterward, General Schwarzkopf simply said to the staff, "we have a lot of work to do, but we also have another corps to work with."

Of course, Generals Schwarzkopf and Powell had spoken many times subsequent to the briefings, and General Schwarzkopf was already at work creating a new ground plan that included the additional corps authorized by the president. Rather than the much maligned high-diddle-diddle-up-the-middle concept, it was a left-hook scheme of maneuver that emphasized speed and shock action that took full advantage of our well-trained troops and our first-class equipment and technology.

General Schwarzkopf had commanders from each of the services under his command: Air Force Lieutenant General Chuck

Horner was his air component commander; Army Lieutenant General John Yeosock was the ground component commander and worked with Lieutenant General Walt Boomer, commander of Marine forces; and Vice Admiral Stan Arthur was the naval commander. Generals Horner and Yeosock were located in Riyadh and were able to attend most meetings with General Schwarzkopf while General Boomer, who was on the Saudi east coast, and Admiral Arthur, who was aboard ship, had representatives there.

As I looked back on it later, I realized something interesting. At the time, CENTCOM was a fairly new combatant command and did not enjoy the high regard or reputation as did European Command or Pacific Command. Those were the commands folks wanted to be assigned to for professional growth, and upward mobility, whereas CENTCOM was viewed at the time as a great place to be assigned for earning your required joint credit for promotion purposes, and more realistically, as a great last tour to precede retirement. Yet the reality was that it was in command of the first major conflict involving U.S. forces since the war in Vietnam.

All the key leaders and its components were proven professionals but, quite frankly, they were probably not slated by their services for future promotions or assignments. General Schwarzkopf had worked with each of these officers during peacetime, and he knew their strengths and weaknesses. He was confident he would be able to bring out the best in each and every one, and mitigate the weaknesses they might have through good leadership on his part and the assistance of others he might bring in for support.

It was a testimony to faith in them that, when it came time to perform, each of these three-stars stood up and did a wonderful job. I was able to watch General Schwarzkopf develop this team into a fully functioning force. What I took away from the situation was a reinforced awareness of the significance of relationships, and the importance of team building and teamwork. The relationship he had with each of these three-star component commanders made things work. Likewise, he knew all the ground commanders of the operational units: Generals Gary Luck, Binnie Peay, Barry McCaffrey, Freddie Franks, Bill Keys and Mike Myatt. He depended on Generals Pagonis, Starling, and Krulak to solve the mammoth logistics challenges.

He was not averse to picking up the phone and talking to any of them if he thought they weren't meeting his taskings or moving fast enough in their preparations for war. Once the ground campaign began, he would not hesitate to call them to get firsthand reports or to inquire as to how they were doing and whether they needed anything in the way of support. Although he didn't know the air commanders as well, he depended upon General Horner to keep him advised and, here again, he did not hesitate to engage if he felt that things were not going as planned. As for advice and support from the coalition leadership, he depended heavily on Lieutenant General Khalid from Saudi Arabia as well as Generals de la Billiere from the U.K. and Roquejeoffre from France.

Any time General Schwarzkopf was taking briefings from which important decisions were to be made, all four component commanders or their representatives were at the table and participated in the discussions. It was participatory leadership at its finest and a healthy atmosphere conducive to good decision making.

I mentioned earlier that the emphasis on joint-service warfighting had been brought about by Congress. It had been germinating for the previous four or five years, and now that it was time to put it into practice, it would end up working pretty well. There were still plenty of things that had to be decided on the fly, which made for some interesting meetings and give and take by all the services. We had to make sure we were optimizing each of the services' capabilities while mitigating their limitations. Any time there was friction or conflict as to the best course of action, it was resolved at the highest level with General Schwarzkopf making the ultimate decision.

The lesson here is the absolute excellence of joint warfare. Just as everyone eventually embraced maneuver warfare, everyone embraced the new model where all the services operated together. The days of going it alone as a service were over, but this did not preclude some lively and parochial discussions throughout the campaign.

Likewise, it behooves all of us to understand the capabilities and limitations of the coalition forces. This was abundantly clear when we saw the professionalism exhibited by our coalition mates who had benefitted from our training mission several years before. It was incredibly satisfying to see that the relationships we had built at that time had stuck—as had the things we had taught our coalition partners.

Being involved in the lead-up to the execution of Desert Storm was like being in a leadership lab as I had the rare opportunity to watch a maestro in action. General Schwarzkopf was challenged with working not only with the highest U.S. political leadership (President Bush, Secretaries Cheney and Baker) and military leadership (Chairman Powell and the Joint Chiefs) but also with the highest military leaders of the coalition forces, including his coalition counterpart, Lieutenant General Khalid from Saudi Arabia. General Schwarzkopf's ability to balance the competing demands from all quarters while at the same time keeping his staff and commanders focused on preparing for war was nothing short of miraculous. I got to see General Schwarzkopf in his finest hours as a leader and commander; a master in action as he developed the coalition into a cohesive team. It was also a unique opportunity to be in a roomful of proven professionals who were all at the two-or-three-star general officer level. The officers in that room brought a wealth of experience and expertise from their military services and the joint community. This was never more apparent than during Desert Shield and Desert Storm.

At the general officer level, we could fall into thinking we were all knowing. Otherwise, we wouldn't be where we were. And we could become resistant to outside input. But a real leader can subject himself to criticism, accept it, and if it seems prudent to do so, take actions to implement the course of action recommended by the owner of a fresh set of eyes; General Schwarzkopf was such a leader. This suited me as I was not a shrinking violet and would comment if I felt things were going in the wrong direction. As I mentioned earlier, we had a great relationship. General Schwarzkopf presented me with a copy of *It Doesn't take a Hero: The Autobiography of General H. Norman Schwarzkopf.* He inscribed with: *To Butch, one of the real heroes of Desert Storm. Thanks.*

Armed with this growing team of professional warfighters and the additional corps we had been given, we basically went back to the drawing board after October and put together a new plan, and this time, General Schwarzkopf was more intimately involved in the planning process. He brought in extra Army folks, most significantly Brigadier General Steve Arnold to lead the planning effort. Forces were flowing into the theater, and the logistics buildup was pretty much on schedule. During this time, General Schwarzkopf was in constant touch with Chairman Powell and occasionally with Secretary Cheney and President Bush.

It is important to note that President Bush had a hands-off approach and let General Schwarzkopf, Secretary Cheney and Chairman Powell run the effort. There is a great book called *The Generals' War* by Michael R. Gordon and General Bernard E. Trainor, USMC (Ret). The book's title reflects the truth: to a large extent, the politicians stayed out of Desert Shield/Desert Storm and let the military plan and fight the battle. Of course, there were times when political participation was critical, as in the case of Secretary of State Baker's monumental efforts in convincing many of the reluctant nations to join the coalition.

It was remarkable that General Schwarzkopf held it all together. It was a blessing to be there and have access as the junior general in the war room, and so beneficial for my professional and personal development.

* * *

We had started deploying forces to the Gulf in August, continued into the theater through December, and pretty much had our late arrival forces in place by January 1st.

There were challenges in keeping the morale up, and we had to break it to the troops that they weren't going to be home for Thanksgiving or Christmas. The time had come, and the clock was ticking down. No one was going home. Instead, we were going to war.

WITH BG JACK LEIDE, THE J-2, BRIEFING MARINES DURING DESERT STORM

CHAPTER 25

DESERT STORM

"Take time to deliberate; but when the time for action arrives, stop thinking and go." --Andrew Jackson

17 JANUARY 1991 – 28 FEBRUARY 1991

RIYADH, SAUDI ARABIA

It was the 17th of January at nearly 0200 when General Schwarzkopf walked into the war room filled with approximately 30 generals, admirals, and key staff. It was a fairly large area with comfortable chairs arranged in a half moon configuration facing mounted screens displaying the latest information; maps, the scheme of maneuver, and status of forces. We also had CNN on almost all of the time. On the built-in desk in front of our chairs were a multitude of phones and communication devices that allowed us to talk to anyone in the world. Between the chairs, desk and screens there was a raised platform from which a seemingly unending stream of briefings were given to the commander and his key staff. Particularly as pertained to the flow of forces into the region, enemy activities, and the building of the coalition.

"Gentlemen..." General Schwarzkopf got our attention and then read a short message that he had just released to the men and women of CENTCOM. "Offensive operations have begun." He had the chaplain say a prayer and then his aide played a tape of Lee Greenwood's song 'God Bless the U.S.A.' At that very moment,

Tomahawk missiles fired from Navy ships were enroute to designated targets in Iraq and Kuwait. And our Special Operations helicopters were crossing the Saudi-Iraq border and attacking two early-warning radar sites. Closely following the helicopter attack were a myriad of aircraft attacking multiple targets throughout Iraq, including targets in downtown Baghdad. The air campaign had begun, and the war was officially underway.

It was a very, very tense time for General Schwarzkopf who used nervous snacking as a means of dealing with the stress. I was busy monitoring calls, talking to the Navy and Air Force, and getting things done; staying focused on what was going on was my way of managing stress. The attack was taking place in parts of Kuwait, and in Iraq miles and miles away. We were too far from the fight to hear the sounds of war—deep underground—and dependent upon status reports.

On pins and needles as we awaited them, thankfully, the reports began to come in almost immediately, and all of them were very positive. Our aircraft were hitting the assigned targets and returning, and the cruise missiles seemed to be going where they were supposed to go. We only lost two planes, an astonishingly low number given that we thought for sure we would lose 75 or more. We were ecstatic over how few losses we sustained.

Later on, the first day, the Iraqis launched seven Scud missiles into Israel. This was a critical move considering that, during the planning for Desert Storm, there was serious concern that Iraq would use Scuds or other means to somehow bring Israel into the war. By doing this, they hoped to fragment the coalition and possibly precipitate its complete unravelling, thereby jeopardizing the war itself.

Though Scuds were unreliable, obsolete Russian missiles, they were effective as a terror weapon and so, reluctantly, we diverted substantial numbers of aircraft from attacking Iraq in order to do

Scud hunting in earnest. The frequency of Scud attacks diminished over time, but the effect of redirecting aircraft from the fight to hunt for their mobile launchers was significant. Chairman Powell deployed an Air Force general to Israel to establish a hotline from there to the war room in Riyadh. He was one of my classmates from the War College, further substantiating the importance of relationships made in the schoolhouse, and he and I spoke all the time throughout the war.

The air campaign continued for three weeks or so, and after all the strategic targets had been taken out by Tomahawks, bombers and strike aircraft, we shifted from strategic targets to tactical targets as we began a systematic shaping of the battlefield in preparation for the ground campaign.

As mentioned previously, General Schwarzkopf had laid out some very specific objectives that had to be accomplished prior to executing the ground war, including the 50 percent reduction of Republican Guard tanks. This and other requirements actually led to one of the few fights between the services, as the Army and the Marine Corps did not feel that General Horner and his air campaign were fully committed to shaping the battlefield as instructed by General Schwarzkopf. Here is where General Waller came to the rescue and inserted himself into the air tasking process to ensure that all service equities were addressed. The shaping campaign continued, while at the same time, ground forces were moving into position for the ground attack.

THE WORDS OF WAR – ENGAGING THE PUBLIC

During the lead-up to the air campaign, folks back in Washington became concerned with how we were handling the public relations piece of the war planning. In fact, there was concern that we had no plan whatsoever for dealing with the media once offensive operations began. The Joint Staff as directed by General Powell sent over a public affairs team to assist the command, which was promptly ignored by General Schwarzkopf, who had not requested them and was not pleased when they showed up.

As the air campaign got underway, it was obvious that the media's appetite was insatiable for news to report, not only for the U.S. public but for the world. Washington knew that we had to feed the beast. Back there, the Pentagon had already initiated a daily briefing on the war for the press, and Chairman Powell told Schwarzkopf to do the same from the theater of operations.

CNN had launched its cable news network about a decade before Desert Shield/Desert Storm but, up until this point, most folks back in the states relied on the three major networks—ABC, NBC, and CBS—for their news. With its around-the-clock broadcasting, CNN completely changed the landscape of American media. Families no longer had to wait for their news to arrive on their doorsteps in the form of the newspaper, or to be broadcast on radio and TV at the appointed news hour. The news was being broadcast directly into the homes of the American public as it was happening, in real time. The families of military personnel fighting in the Vietnam War and World War II certainly had no such luxury. At the time of Desert Storm, CNN was still in its relative infancy and not yet as ubiquitous as it is now, but it would come of age, in large part, due to its on-the-ground reporting from the Persian Gulf by reporters like Peter Arnett and his colleagues, who were on the scene, glued to microphones.

It is important to understand the complications and challenges associated with conducting war with coalition partners, given the transparency created by constant widespread media exposure. This was the first time we had seen war on TV to this extent. We saw a little bit back during the Vietnam War, but this news coverage was different in that it was live and much more comprehensive and broader in scope.

Throughout the war, General Schwarzkopf would go ballistic when major magazines printed maps of our scheme of maneuvers. And the talking heads on TV were saying things like, "Well, it looks like we're going to do a left hook!" We asked ourselves, *where in the hell are they getting this information from?* Lord knows where they got it, whether from speculation or someone in the inner circles of the war planners. In any case, knowledge is power, and needless to say, giving Saddam Hussein this kind of information didn't serve us well.

Right from the outset, Washington was not happy with the folks we had selected to brief the international media, which was growing larger and larger with each passing day. Chairman Powell had a good briefer at the Pentagon in the person of Lieutenant General Tom Kelly, and he wanted someone with the same skills briefing from Saudi, Arabia.

BECOMING 'THE BRIEFER'

We had already been through two or three briefers, and none of them had done the job expected of them. More form than substance, they were not coming across to either the press or the public in a satisfactory manner. They had not demonstrated the ability to stand in front of the international press and answer questions in a forthright and easily digestible manner. The people back in D.C. and both Chairman Powell and General Schwarzkopf were getting frustrated by this time.

Finally, it was decided that we would use General Schwarzkopf's Chief of Staff, Major General Bob Johnson, USMC. He did two or three briefings, and I thought he did a good job, but having him as command briefer was problematic. He had a very demanding billet as chief of staff of the command and just wasn't up to speed on a real-time basis in terms of what was going on operationally. As a result, he was required to spend a lot of precious time preparing before facing the press, and that was time he could ill afford to give up.

General Johnson suggested to General Schwarzkopf, "Why don't we have Butch alternate with me? That way, I can get back to my work. It shouldn't be difficult for Butch since operationally he knows everything and that will save him on prep time."

General Schwarzkopf was hesitant at first. "I don't know Bob, he's running the war room at night and seems to be there most of the day and working with the J-3 staff and coalition command center; I can't afford to spread him too thin."

"Sir, I believe if we alternate as I suggest we can both still do our real jobs."

In the end, he saw the logic of General Johnson's recommendation and agreed to have me try my hand at the briefing.

That first briefing for me was another version of my *What Now, Lieutenant?* moment. No, there were no bullets flying around my head or a crisis to respond to, just a lot of questions from a somewhat hostile group of folks.

RESPONDING TO PRESS CORPS QUESTIONS

Perspiration ran down my back and formed on my forehead as I waited to go before the cameras. Many times, when responding to a question, I was tempted to answer with information that I wasn't completely sure of and hated the idea of saying "I don't know" to questions seen live on TVs around the world. After all, a general is supposed know everything, right? Not so, and I avoided the temptation based on my prior experience as a junior officer; Colonel Julian from my headquarters tour was still with me even after those many years.

After my second briefing, it was General Johnson's turn. I can still remember him walking up to General Schwarzkopf, telling him that he would be doing that night's briefing, and asking if there was anything the general wanted him to stress.

"Why?" General Schwarzkopf asked him. "General Powell likes Butch and believes that we should stick with him as our briefer, so you're off the hook." He looked at me.

I was okay with finding out—that way—that I would be the primary briefer. The best part was that it got me out of the war room. The briefings I conducted were held—above ground—in a hotel across the street. There was a big area already set up, and I would wait on the sidelines until they got ready to broadcast live. Then I would go up to the podium and read my remarks; four or five sentences that had been prepared for me by our public affairs team and approved by General Schwarzkopf. After that, I opened the floor for questions. You never knew what the folks were going to ask you, and quite frankly they ran the gamut:

> "What are you doing to ensure that your bombs aren't negatively affecting the environment?" (This, while the oil wells set on fire by the Iraqis were filling the sky with black smoke!)

> "When do you expect to kick off the ground campaign and are you still coming in from the West?" (Nothing like giving the world our scheme of maneuver!)

> "Are the Marines going to make an amphibious landing into Kuwait similar to their, just concluded, exercise in the southern Gulf?"

I could go on and on with a list of questions that would likely surprise and concern you, as they did me at the time. There were some that always asked questions related to the environment and the effects of bombing and the oil fires on the atmosphere. Others wanted our operational plans right down to the position of forces. Some worried and asked about the food the troops were eating, what kind of boots they were wearing, were they getting their mail and on and on. It was endless, and you just hoped you had the answers to their questions. When I did not, for me and most generals I suspect, replying with "I don't know" was difficult but was the absolutely correct response and one I gave when I had to.

After the first couple of briefings, my confidence grew, and I felt comfortable in front of the TV cameras and the press. When the lights and cameras went off, I would stay and chat with the press for a few minutes, learning their names and gaining their trust. This was along the same lines as eyeball level leadership and helped engender in the press the sense that they could trust me and take what I was saying to the bank. They came to believe that, while they might not always like the answers I gave them, the answers were truthful. If I made a mistake and gave the wrong answer, or they felt I was being evasive or lying, stand by! When faced with difficult questions where I had to say, "I don't know. I'll get back to you." I would always follow through and give them the answer when I found it, which they loved. This, too, also helped me to cement a good relationship with them.

Doing the briefings didn't bother me, and in fact, I welcomed the change of pace. It was out of the ordinary, something completely different from what I had been trained on or what I'd been living with for the previous five months. It was both challenging and exciting at the same time. What made it particularly easy for me was that I already knew everything I needed from an operational point of view, so it wasn't like I had to study hard beforehand. The greatest challenge was avoiding saying something during the brief that might put the troops at risk. But as any professional would or should do, I did prepare. I would spend a couple of hours with the public affairs folks, who would have already been mixing and mingling with the press to find out what current issues most interested them. Based on that information, they would prepare a series of questions to ask me during what we called a murder board. They would play the role of the international media, and throw out questions to prepare me for the briefing.

The beauty of this approach was twofold. It gave me the opportunity in advance of the briefing to be prepared for questions that I did not instinctively know the answers to, and it gave our public affairs team time to research the answers if the need arose. Even more importantly, these murder board sessions got me into a listen and response mode, so that as members of the press asked me questions, I was already framing my response. The last thing you wanted to do as a briefer was to stumble over your words or go silent because you couldn't think of a response.

Perhaps my most difficult briefing took place when on the 13th of February our aircraft struck the Al Firdos bunker in the Baghdad suburbs. Intelligence reports had indicated that it was a command and control site and thus a legitimate target. It is important to note that targeteering is more science than art, and an awful lot of great folks go to great lengths to ensure they get it right before putting something on the target list. Unfortunately, in this case, it was a legitimate target but as we were to find out later some of the Iraqi leadership had moved their families into the bunker complex for safety purposes. As a result, over two hundred civilians were killed by the strike.

General Schwarzkopf did not have any sage advice for me before I headed out to the hotel for this briefing. No doubt he was as concerned as everyone else at the loss of innocent lives while at the same time wondering if we had in fact made a mistake in targeting the bunker. By the time I got to the hotel and was ready to confront the press, the public affairs guy stopped me and said there was an important call I had to take and that they would delay the briefing. Picking up the phone I was connected on a conference call with Chairman Powell and Brent Scowcroft, the President's National Security Advisor, and I believe others. Obviously, all I did was listen as they provided me with the most complete and up to date information they had received on the bunker. Bottom line, it was a legitimate target. The call I received before giving the briefing on the bunker went something like this:

> "Butch, we've checked with all of our intelligence sources and there is no doubt that the bunker was a valid target. Why there were civilians in there we can only speculate, but we've heard from other sensitive sources that the civilians in the bunker were family members of senior Iraqi officers and that they put them in there as a means of protecting them. You need to explain as best you can our deep concern over the loss of innocent lives but at the same time make the legitimacy of the target absolutely clear."

The pictures that hit the TVs around the world were horrendous, and of course, live coverage added to the controversy; the press were like ravenous dogs smelling fresh meat, and they were about to get a perfect serving in the person of General Neal, the briefer. A *What Now, Lieutenant?* it wasn't, but trying to truthfully and completely answer the questions I was about to encounter had my gut stress meter pegged to the right!

Adding to the pressure was the fact that all of our intelligence folks both in Saudi and back in Washington were scrambling to find out what went wrong. As you can imagine, the Iraqis were using every means available to condemn the strike and to use it as leverage to break up the coalition. Fortunately, the coalition was holding firm but everyone, and I mean everyone, was waiting to hear my explanation of the strike.

Armed with this information, I made my way to the podium, read a short statement confirming the legitimacy of the bunker as a target while at the same time lamenting that the Iraqis had put their families at risk, leading to the unfortunate loss of life. Given the continuous TV coverage of dead and wounded women and children being removed from the bunker, the questions—sometimes the same ones but from different reporters—came at me from all quarters and I thought the briefing would never end:

> "General, with all of the intelligence assets we possess, how did you make such a grievous mistake?"

> Me: "The target was a legitimate command and control center, but we have no way of knowing who is inside a target. Believe me, our targeting folks err on the side of caution when it comes to putting a target on the list to be attacked."

> "How many innocent lives were lost?"

> Me: "At this time we have no way of knowing how many civilian casualties there were; remember, this bunker is in Iraq, in enemy territory, and was used as a communications center by the enemy."

> "Is this terrible tragedy going to lead to the breakup of the coalition?"

> Me: "The coalition is strong and though we all regret the loss of innocent lives; we remain committed to the mission of liberating Kuwait."

Finally, and mercifully, it was over. It was obvious that most believed what I said since they had come to know me and trusted that whatever I said was the truth to the best of my knowledge. There were the usual skeptics, and they seemed to enjoy badgering me with question after question trying to somehow trap me into making a mistake or misstatement. I'm sure that I was ten pounds lighter having sweated it out through my socks. I headed back to the war room. As a postscript to the briefing, both the General Schwarzkopf and the folks in Washington were pleased with how the briefing had gone.

* * *

Along with the twenty-four/seven CNN broadcasts, there were also the broadcasts by regular network news channels, as well as the radio transcripts of my news conferences. All of these things combined to make me a household fixture, although I was blissfully unaware of that fact during the war. We did have cable TV in the war room but I never had any real appreciation for the broad reach of the still relatively new cable news stations like CNN until my wife mentioned to me in passing during one of our phone calls, "You don't realize it, but you are everywhere—on TV, radio, and in every newspaper!"

General Schwarzkopf gave the briefings on a handful of occasions when there was an especially significant event or something momentous that needed to be emphasized. He was terrific at it and conveyed a commanding presence, second to none. I kidded him after the Al Firdos briefing, saying, "You always get the easy ones—the Good! But I have to do the Bad and the Ugly. How come?" He pointed to his four stars and we both laughed, indicative of our close relationship.

A few days after that briefing, General Powell called into the war room, and I picked up the commander's phone: "Butch, I need to talk to Schwarzkopf, have someone go get him but stay on the line as I want to talk to you for a second." He paused for a heartbeat. "I want you to know your briefings are worth divisions to me." I believe what he meant by this was that good briefings were invaluable in keeping the public informed about their sons and daughters who were in harm's way and, just as importantly, in keeping the coalition informed about the effort. He viewed strategic communications as being as critical in some respects as the forces in the fight. Then he busted my ego by adding, "Plus, the little old ladies who sit around in tennis shoes, watching TV all day love you!"

I remained the Desert Storm briefer until the end of the war. Because of my time as a briefer, I grew professionally adding greater mental flexibility and an increased ability to be ready for the unexpected. In the context of Desert Storm, I was a brigadier general with no experience briefing the press although, when I was a colonel and the director of AWS, I had observed some public affairs training for the students. Many of the junior officers still saw the press as the enemy, and we tried to divest them of that position by pointing out that the press has a job to do. We pointed out that 90 percent of them were reputable and committed to getting their stories right. Of course, like in any organization or profession, there is the other ten percent that writes whatever they hear without checking the veracity of the story or their source. We wanted junior officers to be cognizant of that fact and also to accept that dealing with the press was something they would experience during their careers, especially in today's media hungry world. Today, all officers, including flag rank officers, undergo public affairs training during their careers as a means of preparing them for such an eventuality. To a large extent, Desert Shield and Desert Storm were responsible for changing the protocol in that regard.

THE GROUND WAR

As we prepared to launch the ground war, the weather was not cooperating, and neither were the forecasters. They kept bouncing around between predictions of rain and high winds or sandstorms. There were many concerns related to both, but the primary one was mechanized forces getting caught in the rain and becoming bogged down as the sand turned to mud and flash flooding reducing mobility and visibility. The weather became a serious factor, much as it did with General Eisenhower in making his D-Day decision.

As the shaping of the battlefield to General Schwarzkopf's satisfaction was being realized, the ground forces moved closer to their jump-off positions, the LOD, and readied themselves for the ground campaign to begin. All the front-line units were ready to go, and the sentiment was, "Let's get this over with! We've been sitting here in this desert since August, and it's almost the end of February." Over those months, they had battled extreme heat, sun, sands, winds, flies and other bugs. Almost to a man and woman, the attitude was, "We're ready... let's get this show on the road!"

They were not the only ones getting impatient. The press and politicians were all wondering aloud, "What are we waiting for?" In addition to concerns over morale and pressure from Washington, General Schwarzkopf also worried that all the waiting could lead to pre-kickoff activity that could prematurely start the ground campaign. He wanted to make sure he was the one to pull the trigger, not the ground forces or the enemy. It was a real leadership challenge to keep everyone focused while waiting for orders to execute ground offensive operations.

The tension stemmed primarily from a fear of the unknown. We didn't know the breadth of the weapons Iraqi forces had and were willing to use—mines, chemicals, gas—and we had no way of knowing how many casualties we would suffer. We believed we had done the best possible job of planning a good concept of operations and scheme of maneuver, but there was simply no way to know in advance what the troops would encounter. Command is not easy. Given the possibility of encountering chemical weapons, our ground forces had to suit up in protection suits. The desert heat along the Saudi/Iraq/Kuwait border where the troops were staged was already taxing, and the addition of the suits made it all the more miserable for them.

The combination of factors created tremendous concern in Washington and generated plenty of conversation between General

Schwarzkopf and General Powell. The pressure was mounting to execute the ground war sooner rather than later. It was President Bush's decision, but he deferred to Secretary Cheney and General Powell, who in turn were determined to leave it to General Schwarzkopf, the on-scene commander. Leaving that decision to him took politics completely out of the process.

On February 24th, the decision was made. General Schwarzkopf felt we had met his conditions to commence ground operations. We hadn't lost the planes we thought we'd lose in the air campaign and everything seemed to be in our favor.

The tension was palpable throughout headquarters when we finally said: "Execute the Order!" As the commander, General Schwarzkopf revisited the anxiety that accompanied kickoff of the air campaign, only it was even more intense this time around because he was an infantry officer who had first experienced ground combat in Vietnam.

As forces moved forward into Kuwait and Iraq during the first 24 hours of the ground campaign, you could sense the stress in the war room like the crackle of static electricity, everyone was on edge. I thought to myself how higher command had been primarily responsible for the tragic decisions that created the circumstances for Getlin's Corner, and I worried that now as a member of such a command whether there was something we had not seen or considered that we should have. In short, *did we plan this right?* General Schwarzkopf had flown out and met with most units before they crossed their LOD. There was a great impact in having General Schwarzkopf on site as the top commander. Old photographs of General Eisenhower meeting paratroopers before D-Day show the same powerful presence. General Schwarzkopf was a ground combat veteran, which gave him a natural affinity for ground forces about to face the unknown.

As the battle unfolded and reports came in from the field, we updated the maps to reflect the situation. What we saw reassured us that–for now–things were going well. General Schwarzkopf was constantly reviewing his execution matrix to see whether his forces were making progress as planned. By monitoring their progress and having the entire scheme of maneuver displayed in front of him, he could best make determinations if he needed to adjust their rate of march to ensure that his forces were synchronized with each other and on target toward meeting their mission objectives.

We watched the entire battle unfold on the map by virtue of the spot reports coming in that gave us a pretty good feel for progress. Sometimes we had to sit there for two or three hours, wondering whether or not we were meeting with success, which was frustrating in the extreme. The waiting never got any easier, but it was made tolerable by the knowledge that the commanders and their troops were busy and would report back when time, circumstances and the enemy situation permitted. General Schwarzkopf and those of us with ground combat experience were especially aware of these factors and their impact on the speed with which the commanders could report back to the war room.

As it turned out, our units moved much faster than our most optimistic expectations. For example, the Marines moved very quickly through their area of responsibility and through the obstacles set up by the Iraqis and were closing on Kuwait City. The coalition forces were moving along the coast and enjoying good success, as well.

Listening to the reports and watching the location of units on the war room maps, General Schwarzkopf knew where all forces were within a few miles. The command had given the Marines and coalition forces the mission to push the Iraqis back while at the same time exposing their forces to Army and British forces attacking from the left against their exposed flank. This was a classic example of maneuver warfare at its finest. The only complicating factor was that the success and rapid progress of the Marines necessitated speeding up the movement of the Army and British forces.

Watching these maneuvers, General Schwarzkopf wanted to make sure forces started the left hook at the proper time to avoid the possibility of friendly forces firing on each other. He continued to push, in one instance putting pressure on one of the commanders who was moving way too slowly from his point of view. The general was in constant communications with him telling him to get moving, that his slow pace was screwing up the scheme of maneuver. If he didn't keep an eye on the big picture, things could get out of synch. Schwarzkopf was conducting a symphony; watching the progress of the battle and determining whether to tell one unit to step up the pace even if it meant it had to move ahead of its timeline. At one point, the Marines were ahead of schedule and he had to order some units to speed up to maintain a seamless front and prevent the enemy from taking advantage of gaps between friendly forces.

THE ROAD TO IRAQ

As we defeated and pushed Iraqi forces out of Kuwait, the main road between Kuwait City and Iraq became the Iraqi forces' main escape route. Hundreds of their vehicles and military equipment were caught on the highway, and our aircraft had a field day attacking them. At first, this action was applauded but after a while, the press named it *The Highway of Death* due to the carnage being shown on TVs around the world. Perceptually, it looked like we were piling onto an inept foe.

As we enjoyed almost unparalleled success with the ground campaign, the question soon arose as to when to end hostilities. Success came so much more quickly than anticipated, and that reality, coupled with fears over anti-Arab perceptions generated by constant cable news broadcasts of the decimation of Iraqi forces, suggested that a cease fire should be in the offing. It was a balancing act to defeat the Iraqis while keeping the coalition together. Even though Iraq had attacked a fellow Arab nation, the coalition was inherently fragile. The coalition had been formed to force Iraq to leave Kuwait. The fact that we were able to assemble this coalition at all was amazing. To ensure that the coalition would not fall apart, we had to be very careful in all of our actions so that we were not perceived as anti-Arab or anti-Muslim. Washington had initially been talking about a five-day ground war, but the success of the forces coupled with televised scenes of the *Highway of Death* created a feeling that, "We've got to wrap this thing up now!" There was talk of stopping it at the hundred-hour mark because it seemed like a nice round number—*The Hundred-Hour War*. From a political and strategic standpoint, the folks in Washington felt that the longer the *Highway of Death* and scenes of our overpowering force continued to appear on cable news and newspapers around the world, the greater the likelihood of the coalition fragmenting.

At the same time, however, General Schwarzkopf was very concerned about a premature cease fire. One of his objectives in the war was the destruction of Republican Guard Forces, and he was not confident that he had achieved that at this point in time. The longer he could keep the fight going, the better the possibility that he could achieve that objective.

Soon, though with some reluctance, General Schwarzkopf agreed that we and the coalition had accomplished our mission by re-establishing Kuwait antebellum—we had pushed the Iraqis out of Kuwait and punished its military. At the hundred-hour mark, all offensive operations ceased, and Desert Storm was over. We were instructed to develop war termination objectives, working in conjunction with Washington. We were also tasked with establishing a location for conducting termination negotiations. After a bit of confusion, we selected Safwan, and it was here that General

Schwarzkopf and General Khalid met with their Iraqi counterparts. The results of the negotiations ending the conflict remain a topic of much discussion, but for CENTCOM and U.S. and coalition forces, it was the end of a hugely successful effort by all concerned.

Desert Storm would go down in history as remarkable in many regards, not the least of which was its distinction as the first major war in American history where events were broadcast in color into every American living room every day. Due to the heightened awareness created by ubiquitous news coverage, we returned home to a public which was better informed than they'd been during Vietnam or any previous war.

THE STORM ENDS AND BRINGS NEW APPRECIATION

The end of Desert Shield/Desert Storm was a cathartic time for the military, and the returning troops were hailed and celebrated as the Great American Military. General Schwarzkopf and many of the forces who served with him were given a parade in Washington, D.C. and a ticker-tape parade in New York City. This was a completely different homecoming from what we experienced when we returned home from Vietnam—a divisive war by any measure. It was a great and well-deserved salute to the young men and women who had served so well in the desert. Reflecting on when I returned from Vietnam to my blue collar-hometown of Hull, people were receptive to those of us who had served our country, regardless of whether they believed the war was right or wrong. My family was proud of me, and the townspeople had accepted my Brothers that returned from the war with me. Likewise, after Desert Shield/Desert Storm, I would return home to Boston and my hometown of Hull to discover that I had become a local hero and something of a celebrity; the Power of the Tube!

CHAPTER 26

AFTER THE STORM

"What lies behind us and what lies before us are tiny matters compared to what lies within us."

--Ralph Waldo Emerson

APRIL 1991

Immediately after the war termination negotiations were concluded, General Schwarzkopf and his staff began the process of redeploying back to Tampa. I knew I would be returning to Washington D.C. to continue my work at Headquarters Marine Corps, but my return date was unknown. At about the same time, I received an invitation to throw out the opening day pitch for the Boston Red Sox. This was the ultimate offer! After all, I was a kid from Boston, and we were talking about the Red Sox. Unbelievable! I am sure that it was thanks to the notoriety as a result of being the CENTCOM briefer that the Boston Red Sox asked me. The fact that I have an easily discernible Boston accent and a degree from Northeastern University didn't hurt, either.

I talked to General Bob Johnson to see if he had any idea when I would be released for redeployment, and discussed the possibility of accepting the invitation. He urged me to speak with General Schwarzkopf. Hat in hand, I went in to meet with the general.

"Sir," I said, "I would like to request that I be allowed to go back home to throw out the opening day pitch for the Boston Red Sox."

He looked at me and feigned great umbrage saying, "Are you crazy? That's your reason for asking to go home? Well, I have an invitation right here from the team that won the World Series!"

"But that doesn't compare to the Boston Red Sox!" I joked.

He followed with a great laugh and responded, "Of course you can." This was further evidence of the great relationship we had developed over the past months.

I simultaneously received a request to give a briefing on Desert Storm at European Command in Brussels. So, I put together a brief, ran it by General Schwarzkopf so he could give his approval and, in April, flew from Riyadh to Germany. Once I had completed the briefing, I took a plane and flew home to Boston.

Returning to the States after a clear victory in Desert Storm was in one word, amazing! I was met at the airport by Kathy and the kids and a whole bunch of relatives. It was an exciting reunion and wonderful to see everyone.

WELCOME HOME

The rapid and decisive victory of Desert Storm created conditions in the country not seen since the end of World War II. Folks just wanted to thank those involved in the effort, and it extended from patriotic songs to parades, to balls and banquets. What a change from the end of the Vietnam War wherein we veterans literally snuck back into the country; there were no parades or 'Thank you for your service' salutations for us back then. For those of us who were Vietnam veterans, it was a most welcome turn of events.

WHITEY BUYS THE BEER

From the airport, we went to Kathy's family home in South Boston. When we got to the house, we realized we were out of beer, so I went over to the local liquor store to pick some up. I put the case of beer on the counter and asked: "How much do I owe you?"

"No charge," said the store clerk who acted like he knew me well. "This one's on Whitey."

I shook my head not understanding, but told him, "Please tell Whitey, thank you!" and left the store with the beer in hand. When I got back to Kathy's family's house, I said, "You won't believe this, but when I went to pay for the beer, the clerk said someone named Whitey was paying for it!"

My sister-in-law Nancy jumped up and said, "Oh, my God! Whitey Bulger bought you the beer? We'll be protected forever!" Until she said that, I hadn't realized that the clerk was referring to the notorious mobster!

Being recognized in the local liquor store after returning home from the war was a testament to the broad reach of cable television and particularly CNN. During Desert Storm, I had no idea that people were now on a steady diet of cable news, being broadcast twenty-four/seven. Kathy had alluded to it during phone calls, and this was reinforced by the large number of letters sent to me from folks around the country.

THE OPENING PITCH

Our whole family was invited to opening day at Fenway Park, and you can just imagine how excited I was to be throwing out the first pitch. I was literally a dyed-in-the-wool Red Sox fan, had attended many games while growing up, and could think of no greater thrill then being selected for such an honor

But I sure was sweating out my throw not having thrown a baseball in some time. I walked out, got in position and let it go. The ball settled in the catcher's mitt, and the crowd went crazy. Folks were screaming from the stands, which were filled to capacity and a lot of the Red Sox players surrounded me congratulating me on the pitch and the success of the military. Wade Boggs, the third baseman, was particularly enthusiastic as he told me he was a military brat and never prouder than he was right then! It was a beautiful spring day.

Vice President Dan Quayle happened to be in the crowd that day, and a representative from the Red Sox team took me over to meet him.

"Good to meet you, Mr. Vice President," I said and shook his hand.

"Great to meet you, General. By the way, I just finished a call with Tipp O'Neill, and he asked me, 'Hey, Danny Boy, are you throwing out the opening day pitch?' I had to tell him, 'Well, no. They had some damn general do it!'"

We shared a great laugh over it. Then I was taken up to the radio announcer's booth. At that point in the game, the Red Sox were losing. The radio announcer asked me, "Well, general, what do you think about the game?"

"They should've left me in!" I said without thinking. It was an offhand remark, but it shot around Boston like a meteorite. Afterward, every blue-collar worker in the Boston area seemed to recognize me on the street. "Hey, general!" they would say with a grin. "They shoulda left you in!"

Soon after that, I was given an Honorary Doctoral Degree from Northeastern University. The great thing about the ceremony was that another Honoree was Barbara Bush, our First Lady at the time; what a wonderful woman. She sent me a picture of the event and signed it "It was an honor to be honored with you." It doesn't get any better than that!

RECEIVING AN HONORARY DOCTORAL DEGREE FROM NORTHEASTERN UNIVERSITY PRESIDENT JACK CURRY, WITH ANOTHER HONOREE, FIRST LADY, BARBARA BUSH

CHAPTER 27

BACK TO MARINE HEADQUARTERS

"There is nothing like returning to a place that remains unchanged to find the ways in which you yourself have altered." --Nelson Mandela

MAY 1991—MAY 1992

WASHINGTON, D.C.

After spending some time with our family and relatives in the Boston area, we returned to D.C. and the house I had never really had a chance to live in. I quickly settled into my daily work routine as head of Manpower Plans and Policies (nine months later than intended). I relished being back with my Marines.

I began receiving an unbelievable number of speaking requests. That's when my notoriety as the briefer really started to sink in. Due to my TV exposure, I was the face of the war. Of course, the real heroes were the men and women in uniform and, although they didn't get the individual attention I did they were warmly received with parades and recognition at public events across the country.

The Marine Corps encouraged me to accept as many of these invitations as I liked. It was a good recruiting tool to have me making public appearances around the country. Throwing out the opening day pitch for the Red Sox may have led to one very special invitation that came about a month after I'd returned to headquarters. I was invited to be a guest conductor for the Boston Symphony Orchestra at the Shell on the Charles on the 4th of July. For this kid from Hull, this invitation was right up there with being asked to throw out the opening day pitch! As thrilled as I was to be receiving such an illustrious invitation, I surprised myself by accepting it. After all, what did I know about conducting an orchestra, particularly one as prestigious as the Boston Symphony Orchestra? Not to mention that I would be doing so in front of thousands of spectators and a national PBS television audience of millions.

WIELDING A CONDUCTOR'S BATON

The producer told me not to worry about a thing. He assured me that the practice session they had arranged for me at Boston's Symphony Hall would get me ready for the big event. I thought to myself, *Yeah, right!*

Somehow, I made it through the rehearsal without incident, donned my summer white uniform, and arrived that evening at the Shell for the big event—or should I say, the moment of truth. The complimentary seats they had provided for my family and relatives were right on the front row, and they had all showed up and were excited about my big moment.

I can't say I shared their excitement. Perhaps scared to death would be a more apt description of my state of mind. In any case, the show went on, and when it was my turn to conduct, I did so with complete abandon and vigor, and a big smile on my face. I conducted *The Stars and Stripes Forever* by John Phillip Sousa (a Marine, I might add), and thankfully the orchestra was on auto-pilot and not distracted by my wild arm movements. In fact, my brother-in-law, Paul, has a videotape of my performance, and he puts all visitors to his ski lodge through the agony of having to watch me in action.

After the show, I linked up with my family, and we headed to a local bar in Hull called Joe's Nautical. It was crowded given the holiday weekend, and we were greeted by many of my longtime, valued friends from Hull. As we were in the midst of trading stories and happenings with each other, a roar arose because right there on the bar TV was a replay of me conducting the orchestra. We all enthusiastically commenced toasting the 4th of July.

SPEAKING & SPEECHES

For the better part of the next two years, I was on what I fondly refer to as the Rubber Chicken Circuit as I traveled around the country, giving speeches. Most of the requests came to my office through the Public Affairs Branch of Headquarters Marine Corps, and they would forward them on for my consideration. It was difficult to turn them down since they were all from great organizations so, for almost two years, I was gone most weekends. One really special request I received during that time was an invitation from the Town of Hull to speak to the Hull High School graduating class. I accepted in a New York minute.

Any time I made an appearance and gave a speech, I was moved by the gratitude expressed to me. I met many young troopers who thanked me and told me that hearing me give my briefings while they were in the desert or aboard ship gave them a sense of comfort and grounded them; I got the same reaction from family members of those deployed. Everyone was so thankful to get updates on what was going on from someone they trusted. And the public obviously loved General Schwarzkopf. There's no question that he was a media star and legitimate military hero. I understood, accepted and relished being in the position of second fiddle to him.

At each event, whether I was speaking to the Rotary Club or at a Marine Corps Birthday Ball, I would go from table to table to meet everyone. I was genuinely interested in what they had to say, and I took the time to let them know it, which was greatly appreciated. People also embraced the fact that I had clearly given thought to my audience when I prepared my speech; I wasn't simply a plug-and-play speaker.

Whenever I spoke in public, I was always careful not to steal General Schwarzkopf's thunder or that of anyone who had contributed to the success of Desert Storm. After all, General Schwarzkopf and his leadership made it all happen. I was his subordinate who did a good job of running the war room at night, and a good job as his replacement in giving briefings. But no one gave as good a briefing as the general. I was always very conscious of that and never strayed from that position.

I learned this important lesson early in my life, and I still embrace and live by it to this day. I always cautioned young aides who were assigned to assist me in my daily tasks not to take themselves seriously, and to avoid at all costs the temptation to feel more important than was appropriate for their station or rank. "Don't start wearing my stars! And don't use my name to get things done! Tell me if you can't get something done and if it's worth pursuing, I will step in to assist." If you're an aide, that's an indication that you're doing well and heading in the right direction. Being an aide does not make you a general, but that doesn't mean you can't become one.

Whenever I speak to young people, I tell them, "It's not the position you're in but rather how you perform in that position. Whatever assignment you may have, it is incumbent upon you to perform it to the best of your abilities and not to concern yourself with what's next. If you want to get to the next level in your career, it's all about performance and recognition by others of your potential for positions of greater responsibility. Grow where you're planted!"

* * *

In 1992, while still assigned to Headquarters Marine Corps, I received orders to Camp Lejeune to be the Deputy Commander of the

2nd Marine Expeditionary Force (II MEF) and also its' Brigade Commander. So, in June, we packed up, headed south and settled into on-base housing.

CHAPTER 28

2ND MARINE EXPEDITIONARY FORCE

"Leadership is the art of getting someone to do something you want done because he wants to do it."

--General Dwight D. Eisenhower

JUNE 1992—AUGUST 1993
CAMP LEJEUNE, NORTH CAROLINA

I was excited about the new assignment as I would once again be with the operating forces and working for the Marine Expeditionary Force (MEF) Commander, Lieutenant General Bill Keys, a close personal and professional friend and longtime mentor to me. In Desert Storm, he was the Second Marine Division commander.

But whenever you're a deputy commander, you are fair game and sometimes you're taken by surprise. That's exactly what happened to me when they were looking for someone to take over a command responsible for a humanitarian relief effort. One day, I was happy as a clam performing deputy tasks and the next moment I was told, "General Neal, pack your bags. You're going to Guantanamo Bay, Cuba to be the commanding officer of Joint Task Force (JTF) Gitmo."

GITMO – JOINT TASK FORCE COMMANDER

During the previous year, droves of Haitian migrants escaping the squalor and political problems associated with Haiti's dysfunctional government headed for the closest American land by boat, which of course was Florida. Our Coast Guard intercepted them on the way to Florida and brought them to Gitmo. Even though the U.S., for many years, had a strained relationship with Cuba, our long-term lease of the Gitmo complex remained in force, and this base provided a convenient location to house the migrants pending resolution as to their final destination. In JTF Gitmo, all of the services were represented up to the rank of colonel, as well as agents from the United States Agency for International Development (USAID), Customs and Immigration, and a whole host of lawyers, medical personnel, and other non-governmental organizations.

Brigadier General Mike Williams, an aviator, and logistician who preceded me, set up a base camp for the migrants on an unused runway at Gitmo. At one point in time, he had over 30,000 Haitians of all ages and medical conditions housed in this temporary camp. This number included babies who had come over with their parents on the boats and some who were born at Gitmo. The fact that these parents were willing to risk subjecting their infants and unborn children to a boat ride into unchartered waters speaks to the terrible conditions they were fleeing.

Mike had done a tremendous job establishing the base camp and setting up the practices and procedures for taking care of the migrants, and I went down there and inherited the fruits of his labor. I had to change certain things and create some new policies but, by and large, he had set the conditions for success. During that tour, we wrote a manual so that, if something like that ever happened again, the commander would be able to use that manual for forming his joint task force without being in the position Mike was in when he started with a blank piece of paper. Sometimes lessons are learned but get lost and have to be relearned. That can be avoided by writing things down.

With a camp population of 15,000 migrants, I felt like the mayor in charge of a small city, and the mission was such that I had to learn by doing. We housed, fed, administered medical treatment, and took care of these migrants, young and old alike, in every possible way. With so many Haitian migrants, it became obvious that we needed to establish some sort of local governance for them. There were cultural puts and takes, as well as language barriers (the Haitians spoke primarily Creole, a hybrid of French and English), and it was decided that it would be to our advantage to have a makeshift town and rules of order. That way, they could bring requests and complaints to us in a common voice. Issues ranged from the type of food we provided, to medical care, to when they would find out when they would be leaving, and most importantly, where they would be going. A lot of our solutions to their issues were born of trial and error but always with what was best for them uppermost in mind.

We quickly determined the need for a second, separate and distinct, camp so that we could quarantine those affected with HIV from the general population. With the help of the Navy's Seabees (units renowned for their construction capabilities), we built a second camp, put the HIV positive migrants and their families there, and treated them with the best medical protocols available. Those infected with HIV were extremely frustrated and understandably so. For one thing, most of them were finding out for the first time that they had a terrible disease. They knew that they were sick but hadn't realized they had a debilitating and potentially fatal disease. And, secondly, they knew that the handwriting was on the wall, and they would ultimately be sent back to Haiti.

We worked overtime to convince these migrants that we were there to help them and pointed out that we had the very best doctors treating them. On one occasion, their frustration had reached a boiling point, and they gathered as a group, protesting their isolation and uncertain future. We made them stand down from their confrontational gathering and return to their living quarters, but we also tried to mitigate their frustration, one born of a loss of hope.

Once the migrants were screened, and it was obvious that they would be returned to Haiti, we turned them over to the Coast Guard to handle their repatriation to Haiti. During the nearly four months I spent at Gitmo, I was able to reduce the population to under 10,000 before I was replaced by an Army general. The migrants as a group tugged at my heartstrings. I felt so badly for them, and especially those who were living with HIV and had little hope. I was painfully aware that, if they were returned to Haiti, they likely would not continue to receive the level of medical care we were giving them. For some, that would be a death sentence.

BACK TO II MEF

I returned to Camp Lejeune and was immediately busy getting organized for another deployment: taking my brigade to Norway for a cold-weather exercise as part of our training to support NATO. We would fall in on prepositioned equipment and exercise with the Norwegian and British forces in cold-weather training.

In advance of the deployment to Norway, we first took the brigade to several locations in the States for cold weather training. We went to the Marine base in the mountains of Bridgeport, California (a base that exists solely for the purpose of conducting cold weather and mountain training). We also took them to Wisconsin and a base in Alaska for further training. Given my time at Gitmo, this was a big climate change for me, and added substance to a lyric from the Marines' hymn, 'We have fought in every clime and place.'

This training was invaluable in acclimating my Marines to operating in extreme cold and preparing them to survive and fight in frigid conditions. In extreme cold, you need the right equipment and to know how to use and maintain it. You quickly realize that everything takes longer to accomplish in such conditions.

I cannot overstate the rigors of operating in a cold weather environment. If you are dealing with just the cold, you have one set of issues, and if there is snow, there is a second set to consider. The training was robust so that if they were called to fight in a cold climate, they understood the dangers associated with the weather. The enemy is one thing, but the weather is another. In war time, one must be highly attuned to the physiological effects of this most unforgiving environment.

When we got to Norway after training stateside, we built a camp that would serve as our base of operations for two or three weeks.

I was fortunate to have a Norwegian battalion assigned to my force, and we were pitted against the British forces. It was snowing hard when the exercise began. I met with my Norwegian counterpart and showed him on my map what I wanted him to do in the exercise.

"As you can see this is where the enemy – the British troops – are located, actually quite close to the fjord."

The Norwegian battalion commander nodded his head. "Yes, it is close, but the terrain looks okay for movement."

"Exactly! I want you to load your men on the boats and motor up the fjord and land here," I pointed to a spot on the map, "and then move quickly inland to flank the enemy forces."

He looked at me, and I could tell he had some reservations. "I don't know, sir. The weather is really terrible, and the water in the fjords can get pretty rough in wind and snow like this."

This maneuver was the best line of attack against the enemy forces. "I understand but believe you can do it. I'll have my force attack here," I indicated another spot on the map, "causing the enemy to defend while you attack their flank. They'll have to react to you, and that will spread them thin. We can roll them up."

"It's a good plan," he nodded but still seemed concerned. "I just worry about the weather."

"I do, too. But I think it actually helps in covering your movement. Look," I told him. "You think about it and discuss with your staff while I step out to make a call." I went outside and walked around in a freezing, damn, blizzard for a few minutes. When I thought I'd given him enough time I went back inside.

He looked up from the map as I approached him. "We discussed and believe it's a good plan. It's an acceptable maneuver, and we will accomplish the mission you've given us."

"Great!" I said. "Let me know when you're ready to go and we'll synchronize the attack. Good luck!"

Not long after this we launched the attack and that's when the weather got considerably worse. The wind, even thicker with ice and snow, was gale strength. The mostly narrow fjords became a flue that concentrated and channeled the wind, intensifying it. Suddenly, I had a knot in my stomach like the one I had as I watched the overloaded medevac helo lift off, almost 25 years ago, at Getlin's Corner. I worried that my Norwegian forces would be scuttled in the fjord, and people would be lost or injured. That is exactly why my Norwegian counterpart had hesitated to agree. Thankfully, and to my great relief, the Norwegian forces executed the maneuver to perfection, surprised the British forces and captured most of their equipment. I was one happy commander.

Upon our return to Camp Lejeune, I resumed my usual but satisfying responsibilities as deputy to the MEF Commander. Since, General Keys was spending most of his time at his other headquarters in Norfolk, Virginia, I was pretty much my own boss and enjoyed free rein and his complete confidence. I conducted most of the evaluations for deploying units and handled any other task General Keys assigned. And, like any deputy, I was out in the field a lot, observing the units as they conducted their training. I appreciated the opportunity to see young Marines and their commanders performing their training, ever aware that they could be deployed on operational missions at any given moment.

I really enjoyed every moment as the deputy, but upon notification that I had been selected for promotion to major general, I was eager to learn the details of my next assignment.

CHAPTER 29

COMMANDING GENERAL, 2ND MARINE DIVISION

"I don't run a democracy. I train troops to defend democracy and I happen to be their surrogate father and mother as well as their commanding general."

--Major General Al Gray, CG 2nd Marine Division

APRIL 1993—AUGUST 1994

LIVING THE DREAM

Shortly after I was selected for promotion, I was notified that I would remain at Camp Lejeune, assigned as the Commanding General of the 2nd Marine Division. That I was ecstatic would be an understatement; it couldn't get any better than that.

The disappointment I had always felt over not being selected for the infantry at TBS was finally mitigated by this assignment. Taking command of a Marine division, the ultimate warfighting organization in the Marine Corps; an opportunity to command, lead, train and mentor over nineteen thousand Marines and sailors, in a word was... awesome!

One of the first things I did after the change of command was to have an 'Officers Call' in the base theater for all division officers not deployed. My purpose was to share with them two things, my expectations of them and what they could expect from me. My expectations were that they:

- Develop Subordinates
- Manage Expectations
- Communicate | Coordinate | Cooperate
- Be Their Own Toughest Critic
- Learn to Delegate
- Don't Hide Behind Their Computer

I made sure they understood my commitment to eyeball level leadership and made it clear they were expected to embrace it too with the men and women under them. I restated the absolute requirement for each of them to meet the demands of personal and professional accountability and responsibility in everything they did, and that I would accept no less. Instinctively I felt this was the right thing to do. People always like to know, *what is the boss interested in? What does he expect of me? How does he operate?* I was certain that I had answered these questions. Similarly, I followed this meeting with one with my senior enlisted leaders. Everyone now knew where I stood, what was important to me, and how I operated.

It had a settling influence throughout the command and set the table for what was to come. A few times you could hear people gasp when I advised some actions that might be construed as out of the ordinary. For example, I suggested that at 1400 hours on Friday afternoons, when they had been out in the field for the past five days or so and returned to base; once all gear had been cleaned and inventoried, officers should consider forming a 'school circle' to tell their Marines how pleased they were with their performance and then sound the liberty bell. Letting them go that early sounded like a heretical action to some, but for those who understood command climate and eyeball level leadership, it was a welcome approach.

The responsibilities associated with being a division commander were all-encompassing. Not only was I responsible for ensuring that the men and women under my command were all well led, trained, equipped and ready to deploy at a moment's notice, but I was also, for all intents and purposes, their surrogate parent. It is no exaggeration when I say that I was responsible for providing for their housing, feeding, medical, safety and discipline but my responsibilities didn't stop there. Though most of them were young and single, I had many who were married, separated, divorced or single parents and these presented their own unique challenges to my leadership team and me. We had a lot of balls in the air at any one time but, make no mistake, this is what command is all about. This is what every leader yearns for throughout his or her career.

TALKING WITH COLONEL BILL COLLOPY, WHO HAD BEEN A LANCE CORPORAL IN INDIA 3/9

Just as they were earlier in my career, the mess halls (now called dining facilities) were still one of my favorite areas of focus. I am a firm believer that starting the day with a good meal is critical to a good command climate. So, each morning at 0500, I showed up at one of the many mess halls belonging to me to make sure they were open on time and food was ready for the troops. It was important to me that the food was hot and ready to eat when my Marines came through the door. When my mess hall visits became common knowledge within the division, and my officers found out what I was doing, they started to pay attention, as well. If the boss was interested, it trickled down, and the leaders under them become involved.

Likewise, most evenings, as part and parcel of my leadership style, I inspected at least one barracks. I was not looking for dust balls or 'Gotcha!' issues. Walking through the barracks in the evening, so the men and women could see me and feel my presence, paid great dividends and contributed to good order and discipline and I learned a lot about the command climate. It allowed me to get a sense of the unit and determine whether it was heading in the right direction, the opposite direction, or standing still. With enough experience, it's easy to pick up on these things.

Any time I spoke with the troops, which I did on a routine basis, I made sure the conversation extended beyond military issues of training, equipment, and troop complaints. I would often take the opportunity to ask my Marines, "What do you think of this activity?" Or, "Is there a better way of conducting this task?" I asked them if they were married, whether their families were living on base or off, how they liked where they were living, how their wife and kids were doing, whether the medical care they were receiving was adequate, whether their wife was stuck at home without an automobile, and things of that nature. Their answers to these questions gave me the pulse of the command and facilitated the initiation of corrective action when and where required.

Many leaders are uncomfortable mixing and mingling with the Marines that work for them and are more inclined to let the junior officers and enlisted non-commissioned officers handle that responsibility. Unfortunately, they have fallen into the trap of hiding in their office behind a computer, considering themselves good commanders simply because they have a computer and are abreast of what is going on. I found that engaged and involved leadership extends to all ranks and fosters a good atmosphere and great working environment.

While some will tell you that an officer shouldn't be out banging around the mess halls or barracks because those are senior enlisted responsibilities, I strongly disagree. For me, the only way to be an effective, responsible leader is through engaged leadership. Of course, there is a fine line that must be recognized between officers and enlisted. The nature of the jobs and responsibilities we all have makes that separation necessary—but that doesn't mean that there has to be a red line. This is a nuanced gray area, and common sense tells you when it makes good leadership sense to hold that line and when you can bend a little. Having that leadership sense often means the difference between real leaders and those who don't measure up.

Many young officers, particularly lieutenants, just want to be accepted and liked by their Marines, which sometimes leads them to overstep the line. As mentioned previously, being young and short on experience they tend to operate in a black and white world. They view things in absolute terms, and there is no middle ground—people are either guilty or innocent, good or bad, right or wrong. Consideration of facts that might better explain an issue is left unaddressed, giving rise to flawed judgments and improper or wrong conclusions. It is only after officers gain more experience in dealing with their Marines that they begin to see events in less absolute terms. They learn to accept that there might indeed be facts of extenuation and mitigation that should be taken into consideration before passing judgment or making a decision.

As I had risen through the ranks, I increasingly realized the weakness, and shortsightedness, of a superficial approach. I learned that if there's a problem, you should dig deeper than, "He's late for work, let's write him up!" As your experience and education expands, hopefully, it translates into wisdom in dealing with people, and prompts you to ask questions like, "What caused this action with this young Marine? Did his car break down? Did his wife run off with his buddy? Is a member of his family in the hospital?" Greater experience and education make you more likely to open the lens on a particular problem and take all the facts into consideration. Maybe the staff sergeant needs to talk to Pfc. Jones, find out what his problem is, and see if there's anything he can do to help him. When the moment arrives that a lieutenant—or any officer or senior enlisted—can step back and consider all the facts before making a decision, then he or she has truly become a leader.

BEING READY WHEN OTHERS ARE NOT

The pace of day to day activities for the division was eye watering. Units were training all the time, either in preparation for deployment or upon returning from deployment. In Camp Lejeune's training areas, there was constant activity as units trained five to six days a week. The training ran the gamut from live-fire shoots, wherein the Marines fired their weapons and experienced tank, artillery and crew-served weapons fired in support of their movement, to combat in a built-up area, to patrolling, to squad and platoon tactics. We were limited only by imagination and initiative, and I encouraged my commanders to conduct their training in as realistic a manner as possible. Readiness was the critical element in all that we did— readiness to complete whatever mission might be assigned in a professional and thorough manner.

I spent the majority of my time out with the units, observing their training and taking as much time as possible to engage with them, asking questions. Whenever I had the opportunity, I emphasized to the young, non-commissioned officers—those corporals and sergeants in my command—the importance of engaged leadership with their troops and I was always amazed at their receptivity to it.

Marines pride themselves that they are most ready when the nation is least ready. To this end, physical fitness plays a large role in our day to day activities, and I am a firm subscriber to fitness and an avid runner. Every week during my time as division commander, I would take the people from headquarters out for a run. Not only was it an opportunity to get out of the office and do some physical training, but my staff and I became a visible presence as we ran in formation throughout the base. I usually did this on Friday mornings before weekend liberty, and it proved to be a great motivator for the staff and the rest of the command. Soon, all the units in the division were out there with us.

While we were on one of these runs, my aide, Lt. Todd Desgrosseilliers, and I came up with the idea for a 'Burn the General Run,' an event that I knew would be a lot of fun, create excitement in the division, and drive home my engaged leadership style. What better way to fire up the troops than to appeal to their competitive spirit? Marines love competition—it's in their blood—so I figured that racing against and trying to beat the 'old man' would be well received. But I had no idea what an overwhelming response I would get.

We made a course three miles long (matching the distance of our Marine Corps standard physical fitness test) that traversed the base. The day of the race we closed off roads, and military police made sure we didn't get run over. It was all very well organized by our Special Services folks. The race would end inside the base football stadium where we would hold a ceremony to award certificates to those who 'burned the General' and offered 'I was burned by the General!' certificates to those who were less successful.

There was no shortage of individual Marines and units that signed up; it seemed the whole damned division wanted to Burn the

General! Three thousand turned out and the race became very spirited.

United States Marine Corps

Awarded to _____

for having successfully "Burned the General" during the Commanding General's "Burn the General Run".

given at

2D Marine Division, MarForLant

Camp Lejeune, North Carolina

this _____ day of _____ 19 ___

BURNED THE GENERAL CERTIFICATE

At the starting line, standing just in front of me, was a sergeant. He looked over his shoulder at me, patted his right hip and smiled. "General, I got you in my pocket!" His grin broadened, "I'll dust you."

"No way I'm gonna settle for a, 'I got burned by the general,' certificate!" I overheard two Marines talking.

At the end – the finish line – I was greeted by a young Marine, who had finished ahead of me. "General, I've been here for five minutes. Did you stop for lunch?"

And another young man grinned at me. "General, you beat my commanding officer; you the Man!"

When all had finished the race, the 2nd Marine Division Band played and we had a cookout. It was a gala atmosphere, and the troops just loved it.

One of my favorite memories perfectly illustrates what I consider leadership to be. It involved a young Marine with a bit of a pot belly—not something one should ever see on a Marine. I was inspecting his uniform and stuck a finger in his belly, saying, "Is that my good Marine Corps chow, Pfc?"

"No, sir," he replied candidly. "That's Domino's Pizza free delivery."

I asked him, "That's great, how'd you do on your last physical fitness test?"

"275, sir!"

With a top score of 300 on the test, all I could say was, "Keep eating pizza, Marine," I nodded at him and moved on to the next man. He—that Marine—wasn't a wise ass; he was just giving me an honest answer. Could you imagine saying that to a general? That was a testament to my eyeball level leadership and the climate it created. Engaged leadership breaks down barriers quickly, allows both parties to feel comfortable, and plants the seeds for a good relationship. People felt like they could open up and talk to me.

I also had units spread around the world, from those at sea in the Mediterranean and the Arabian Gulf, to those in Okinawa for a six-month deployment, to units in California doing cold weather training at Bridgeport or desert training at Twenty-Nine Palms, to those at Fort Bragg in North Carolina conducting artillery training.

For nearly two years, I lived and breathed this assignment and was committed to doing whatever it took to prepare my Marines and their leaders for whatever mission might come their way. My reference point was my *What Now, Lieutenant?* moment those many years ago. With that experience serving as my guide, I committed my time, energy and enthusiasm to my responsibilities as division commanding general.

In the midst of my euphoria as division commander, I got a phone call from Headquarters Marine Corps, advising me I had been nominated to be the Deputy Commander at U.S. Central Command in Tampa. Even though the other services were asked to nominate for the position, Headquarters was pretty sure that I would get it based on my two previous tours with CENTCOM.

CHAPTER 30

JOINT AGAIN | U.S. CENTRAL COMMAND

"What you do...
Still betters what is done."
--Shakespeare

AUGUST 1994—SEPTEMBER 1996

MACDILL AIR FORCE BASE

TAMPA, FLORIDA

I was surprised, considering that I had been a two-star general for less than two years, and this new position was a three-star assignment. Truthfully, I had mixed emotions about the nomination. I thought to myself, *Sure, being promoted to three stars would be great but having to give up command of the division before completing a full tour would be disappointing.* I sincerely felt that I had more to do with the division and, of course, my job satisfaction was off the charts. Nevertheless, my past experience made me comfortable that, if selected, I would enjoy being back at CENTCOM and helping the command tackle the seemingly endless issues associated with countries in the Middle East.

Shortly after that call, I was notified I had indeed been selected for the assignment and would be promoted to Lieutenant General. Kathy and I started the difficult process of saying goodbye to the many friends we had made at Camp Lejeune and specifically in the division. Once again, we packed up and headed south.

Fortunately, there was a designated house on base for us to quickly move into but here again Kathy was challenged with getting one more house organized. Our children had grown up; Erin was able to spend her summer break with us, but then she had to return to college. Amy had graduated from college by now, so she decided to stay with us and began job hunting in the area. Andrew was busy teaching at a junior college in Maryland while at the same time pursuing his master's degree.

Settling into my role as deputy commander was pretty easy since I had previously spent three years in the command as a colonel and knew how things were done. Of course, there had been many changes as a result of Desert Storm, and now CENTCOM was viewed as the command with perhaps the most important mission when compared to the other combatant commands. The region of the world for which the command was responsible was less stable than we had hoped after the war.

My new boss was General Binney Peay, an Army four-star who had commanded the 101st Air Assault Division during Desert Storm and was recognized as a true warfighting professional. [Remember as a joint command, it was common for the commander to be from one service, and his deputy to be from another service.] General Peay had a low-key personality but, by virtue of his intellect, his education, and his experience, he possessed great wisdom. He was a true gentleman and epitomized my idea of a quiet professional; a natural leader, teacher, and mentor. My introductory discussion with him convinced me that this was going to be a great tour of duty:

"Butch, I chose you because of your record and based on calls I had with your Commandant, General Mundy, Lieutenant General Keys and General Schwarzkopf."

"Thank you for the opportunity, sir," I replied. "I have to admit that I hate giving up the division, but I look forward to working with you and the staff. It's going to feel like 'old home' week to me."

"You have more experience and expertise on this part of the world than anyone and I'm going to rely on you to give me advice on dealing with the different countries."

"You can count on me."

"My intent is to make sure you know what I'm thinking, planning and attempting to do." He paused then continued. "No holdbacks and no secrets, as I trust you and your instincts."

* * *

As his deputy, I did whatever he asked me to do while at the same time trying to take as much off his plate as possible so he could focus on the big issues. The chemistry between us was superb, we liked and complemented each other, there were no secrets, and we relied on each other to meet the mission. I would go in, open up the place, check his agenda to see what he was doing that day, and then craft my day around his. He traveled to the Middle East quite a bit, and would be gone two or three weeks at a time. Just before his first trip while I was his deputy he called me to his office, "Butch, you run this place while I'm gone. You enjoy my complete confidence and trust."

To ensure continuity of effort, he invited me to all of his briefings, always took extra time to keep me abreast of telephone conversations or messages he thought I should be aware of, and actively solicited my ideas and opinions on just about every issue. We enjoyed a great personal and professional relationship based on trust.

It was during my first year as deputy that Iraq started to show signs by action and deed that the Son of Desert Storm might be in the offing. As the situation in the Middle East deteriorated, the decision was made to deploy a Forward Headquarters element to Saudi Arabia as a signal that the United States was not going to sit idly by while Iraq engaged in such provocative actions. I was designated as

216

the commander of CENTCOM Forward and, armed with a small staff, we loaded onto a plane at MacDill Air Force Base and deployed to Riyadh.

It was *déjà vu* as I found myself in my old stomping grounds, a place so familiar it felt as if I had never left three years earlier. Fortunately, Brigadier General Matt Broderick had arrived before me and *persuaded* the Saudis to allow us to occupy a portion of our former Desert Storm Headquarters. I still had relationships with many of the same people I had known when we were there previously. In many respects, it was a walk down memory lane as I dusted off my recollections, good and bad, of what I had seen and heard during Desert Shield/Storm.

Getting organized as a fully functioning headquarters was much easier to do the second time around as we knew who to ask for help, where to plug in the equipment, and where to feed and house the troops. We were up and running in short order and ready to conduct offensive air operations, should the decision be made to do so.

It seemed as if our quick deterrent actions had the desired effect and the rumblings in the area failed to materialize into anything. However, the real beauty of the deployment was the signal it sent to the region that we were serious in our commitment to do whatever it took to support and protect our friends and allies. Likewise, it was a valuable training mission for our headquarters as it allowed us to dust off our deployment and employment practices and procedures, something we hadn't done for some time.

We stayed for several months then redeployed back to Tampa. Not too long afterwards, a tragic incident occurred. In June of 1996, a bomb went off at Khobar Towers in Dhahran, which housed U.S. Air Force members operating out of Saudi Arabia. There were nineteen killed and approximately five hundred wounded; the loss of life and shock of such an attack was unbelievable. The Secretary of

Defense formed a task force to investigate the incident to find out how and why it had happened. Specifically, the task force was challenged to explore the adequacy of the security there, the division of responsibility for that security, and the sufficiency and effectiveness of intelligence—and then to recommend actions that would preclude such an attack from ever occurring again.

This bombing brought back memories of the Beirut bombing while I was a battalion commander at Camp Lejeune. At the time, the same questions were being asked: was it the European commander's responsibility or the on-scene Marine commander's. The finger-pointing and the investigation that followed that tragedy were just as intense as what was then happening at CENTCOM.

I'm not sure they ever completely proved who was responsible in that incident. In any case, this terrible tragedy resulted in CENTCOM being put under the microscope. A lot of politicians jumped in, asking, "How could this happen? Whose responsibility, was it?" And all the talking heads on CNN piled on too, speculating about how such a thing could have happened. Obviously, it was a traumatic time in the command. We dedicated a lot of time to investigating and dissecting what had occurred. The task force came down and reviewed all relevant documents associated with Khobar Towers, from intelligence reports to installation inspection reports, to security assessments, and they also conducted interviews with General Peay and involved key staff. General Peay left no stone unturned in his efforts to meet the task force's requirements while at the same time continuing his demanding schedule associated with being responsible for over twenty countries in the region.

I watched the process and was reasonably satisfied it was fair and all inclusive, although I had my concerns that the task force never really understood the command relationship between the service component commander and our command. While General Peay was responsible for the *countries* in the region, the component commander was responsible for his forces deployed there, from housing to feeding, to security to discipline. Overall, the report from the task force was fair and balanced and, most important, introduced our nation and its military to terrorism as a form of warfare labeled as a 'weapon of the weak.' The incident was a real kick in the stomach for such a proud and wonderful general, but he never missed a beat in meeting the challenges associated with his position. The fact that we were such good friends made this whole incident all the more difficult from my point of view. I hated to see him suffering and felt his pain.

One evening while all of this was going on, Kathy got a surprise call at home. It was General Charles Krulak, Commandant of the Marine Corps.

"I hope you're going to like coming back to Washington D.C.," he said.

"What? We're not coming back to D.C.!" Kathy said. She was quite happy with our Florida tour.

"Ahh, well," he said, laughing a little bit. "I'm not so sure about that. Where's Butch?"

"He's out... I'll have him call as soon as he gets in."

When I got home, Kathy said to me, "General Krulak called. He says we're going to Washington!"

"Nah," I said to my wife. "Let's just wait and see what he has to say." I wasn't sure why General Krulak wanted to talk to me, but assumed the call pertained to another three-star position he wanted me to fill in D.C.

Before returning the call, I gave serious thought to telling him that, while I was honored he wanted me for another job in Washington, I felt duty bound to stay to assist in wrapping up the demands of the task force. I didn't want to leave General Peay during this most stressful time for him and the command, but when he and I discussed it, he was excited for me and wouldn't hear of me turning down another assignment to stay with him. I suspected that General Krulak had spoken with General Peay, and already knew the exact nature of my new assignment before I did.

I called General Krulak that evening. When he answered, he didn't make any small talk. "Butch, I want to bring you to D.C. as my assistant commandant." I was silent with surprise and shock. He didn't wait for me to speak and continued. "You may be surprised by the assignment. Don't be. Everyone I consulted about you had nothing but great things to say; loyalty, integrity, and moral courage were the words most used in describing you." He paused then continued, "Making this decision, I knew you and I didn't share the same circle of friends. And I think some of yours don't have the highest regard for me." He flat out said, "I'm concerned that their impression will affect yours of me."

I immediately responded, "Sir, if you bring me on, no one, and I mean no one, will be more loyal to you or our Corps than me." History will bear out the fact that I was true to my word. To say I was flabbergasted over his selection of me is an understatement. It was, at the time, an unwritten rule that the position of ACMC was generally reserved for an aviator. The Commandant of the Marine Corps had always been a ground officer, and in order to give aviators a shot at four-stars, somewhere along the line, it became customary to select one to be the ACMC. Of course, this was not always the case, but for the most part, it was an unwritten policy that most commandants tried to adhere to, hence my surprise over his selection of me for the position.

I suspect that General Keys might have been instrumental, to a fair degree, in convincing General Krulak to take a real hard look at me for his assistant commandant. I had worked for General Keys at II MEF, and as his 2nd Division Commander, and suspect that, if he had a 'little black book' of promising Marines to keep an eye on, he might have put my name in it. [Army General George Marshall of World War II fame was notorious for having a similar little black book from which he selected Generals Eisenhower and Bradley, as well as other leaders for the war.] General Krulak had great respect for General Keys and knew that, if he was recommending me over everyone at the general officer level in the Marine Corps, he should take the recommendation to heart.

I have no way of knowing whether a recommendation from General Keys tipped the scales in my favor. I am sure, however, that General Krulak looked at all eligible three-star generals in the Marine Corps. At the time, there were only about a dozen three-stars from which to choose. He no doubt set down on paper a list of candidates, and he surely had his own opinion of each of us. He undoubtedly called General Peay and asked, "How is Butch doing?" I'm also sure General Krulak spoke with other senior officers with three-stars working for them.

Only General Krulak knows the reason he selected me. I suspect that much like General Wilson did when selecting General Jaskilka, he saw merit in what I brought to the position and believed I possessed some complementary skill sets. He was willing to buck tradition and move in a different direction in order to make sure he met the needs of the Marine Corps with a team he felt would work well with him.

As for me, life was coming full circle. All those years ago, after the Battle of Getlin's Corner, it was General Krulak's dad, Lieutenant General Victor Krulak, who, as commander of Fleet Marine Forces Pacific, signed my Silver Star award citation for my actions on March 30–31st, 1967. Now I was going to work with his son.

When I concluded the call with General Krulak, I sat for some time in my home office, thinking about what had just occurred. Remarkably, I was going to be nominated to be the Assistant

Commandant of the Marine Corps (ACMC) and promoted to four stars!

Of course, the process still had a ways to go. First, the Secretary of the Navy had to agree with General Krulak's selection of me and forward the recommendation to the Secretary of Defense. Then he had to agree and forward the recommendation to the President of the United States—who then had to submit my name to the U.S. Senate as the nominee for the position and promotion to four stars. The U.S. Senate, in turn, had to schedule a confirmation hearing or vote and only once I was approved would it be a done deal.

I knew that this could be a long process. More importantly, I was asking myself, *My God, am I up to the task?* I had been promoted only five years earlier to brigadier general, and now I was being recommended for promotion to general and four stars. It is noteworthy that the assistant commandant and commandant are the only two four-star opportunities within the Marine Corps. The assistant commandant position is a two-year position while the commandant serves for four years. This staggered assignment procedure allows for continuity of effort in supporting the commandant and the Corps. With the growth of joint assignments, the opportunity for additional general officers has improved dramatically. Each of the services can nominate for these joint positions when they become available thus increasing promotion possibilities. The Marine Corps has done exceptionally well in being able to promote additional generals to four-star rank. Significantly, the Marine Corps—as small as it is—had five four-star generals at one time. This is indicative of the quality of our officer corps.

I sat there and reflected on all that had transpired since I was pinned with my first star. During the previous five years or so, I had been the deputy to several great military leaders and professionals. How lucky could someone be to have had the opportunity to work with such tremendous warfighters, leaders, and mentors? I learned so much from all of them and each in their own way helped me to grow professionally and personally. I could only imagine that it was the endorsement from these folks that helped influence General Krulak's decision.

As I wrapped up my assignment under General Peay, I spoke with him about it. We sat in my office one of my last afternoon's working for him. "Your experience, contacts, and constant study of your profession have given you great wisdom. I hate to see you go, but I'm so proud to see you get your fourth star." He slapped me on the back. "You've earned it, Butch. The trust you develop in others and that they see in you, is your greatest strength."

* * *

From the time I got General Krulak's call, I had exactly a month and a half to step down, get my replacement settled in, and start moving our household effects. Meanwhile, the Marine Corps was getting the Washington, D.C. house that is designated for the assistant commandant prepared for us to move in. Our new home was a beauty, located at the corner of 8th and I Streets on Capitol Hill. It was situated in a quadrangle comprised of quarters and barracks known historically as Marine Barracks, Washington D.C.

Here, in addition to our home, was the Home of the Commandant and several other general officers' quarters as well as the barracks for those Marines that supported all the military requirements in the region. From security duty at the White House and Camp David to burial details at Arlington National Cemetery, to being the home of the President's Own Band (comprised entirely of an elite group of Marine musicians, all of whom have either masters or doctorate degrees). The young Marines stationed there were always on the go. This patch of land in the middle of the city would be our home and neighborhood for the next two years.

CHAPTER 31

ASSISTANT COMMANDANT, U.S. MARINE CORPS

"If you don't know where you are going, any road will take you there." --George Harrison

SEPTEMBER 1996—NOVEMBER 1998

WASHINGTON, D.C.

I flew up to D.C. ahead of Kathy and reported to Headquarters Marine Corps. In order to facilitate a smooth transition, I wanted to spend as much time as possible with General Rich Hearney before he stepped down as the current ACMC and I assumed all responsibilities associated with the position. I had not really spent much time at headquarters during my career, so I had some serious concerns. They stemmed from the fact that, while most of the folks at the Pentagon had done multiple tours there, I had not. During my 1975 to 1978 assignment at Headquarters Marine Corps (HQMC), the headquarters was located in the Navy Annex. It wasn't until after my tour of duty there as a brigadier general that HQMC moved to the Pentagon.

Typically, one would do a Pentagon tour as a full colonel or a one-star, two-star, or three-star general. Had I ever done a tour at that level, I would have walked into the Pentagon as an ACMC already in possession of greater knowledge where all the Marine Corps staff worked and would have known where to go to address issues—who to see and talk to. Of equal import was knowing how to navigate around that vast 5-sided building without getting lost.

Funny enough, I had always taken bragging rights over the fact that I had, for the most part, managed to stay away from headquarters. To my way of thinking, staying away from it throughout most of my career meant I was basically doing what Marines were supposed to be doing. As a Marine Officer, I always felt I should be with my Marines in the field. Some guys thought they could get ahead by being near the flagpole, thereby increasing their likelihood of being recognized by the leadership, but that wasn't my thinking.

I believe that the reason General Krulak was unconcerned with my lack of headquarters time and experience was simple: he had well in hand the programmatic issues he wanted to accomplish. By selecting me, he probably saw someone with solid operational and valuable joint duty experience, someone who would 'carry the water' on those tough issues he wanted us to fight for. And finally, someone who was unafraid to tell him when he was wrong. After all, I had been a deputy three times since becoming a general officer, and I'm certain he queried my former bosses as to my performance of duty and loyalty to their programs.

Upon my arrival, I had only a broad sense of what my role as ACMC might encompass. First and foremost, I intended in every way possible to make General Krulak's job easier and handle whatever tasks he assigned to me. At the same time, I was intent on meeting the demands in those areas specifically identified as my responsibility. General Hearney did a great job of identifying my specific roles and responsibilities as ACMC and gave me a lot of invaluable advice concerning working with General Krulak and my counterparts in the other services. His efforts made for a smooth transition and considerably reduced my anxiety and trepidation over this new and challenging assignment.

Once the changeover was complete, I flew back to Florida to assist Kathy in making the move. Truthfully, when Kathy had first heard that we were leaving Florida for D.C., she wasn't too happy. We had made a lot of friends while in Florida and could not have been more blessed than having General Peay and his wife Pam as neighbors and special friends. Adding to her concern was her knowledge of the significant—daunting—social responsibilities that went along with being at headquarters as the wife of the assistant commandant. On the upside, she was familiar with D.C., and the move did bring us closer to Andrew and Erin, who were both living and working in Maryland at the time.

We knew we would be on the Washington social circuit and attending many functions throughout the area. Kathy knew that she was an integral part of the team, and I couldn't have done it without her. The number of functions, balls and ceremonies she attended with me are too numerous to tell. And, every Friday night during the summertime, there was a parade right outside our home on the parade deck within the quadrangle, with about five thousand in attendance. We hosted many of them, usually with an honored guest that the Marine Corps wanted to recognize. Each event was special and usually preceded by a reception, either in our home or the barracks band hall. The Marines would march on, usually accompanied by the Marine Corps Drum and Bugle Corps and the renowned Silent Drill Team. Each and every time, the performance was flawless and the pride I felt in being a part of this outfit called the Marine Corps was profound.

Very soon after my arrival, General Krulak and I sat down to go over the issues confronting the Marine Corps over the next few years to ensure that I had a good grasp of our position relative to each of them. He was generous with his time and went out of his way to make me comfortable.

"These are the issues and challenges you and I will face in the next two years." He leaned back in his chair, looking at me over his desk, and held up the index finger of his right hand. "The most important item on our agenda is keeping the Bell Boeing V-22 Osprey program on track. I'll work the Hill—Congress—and you will as well. Inside this building—the Pentagon—I need you to continue to push your counterparts to support the program." He raised a second finger, "Implementing the newly approved *Don't Ask, Don't Tell* Policy and addressing proposed changes in the services Fraternization Policy, on that..." he leaned forward to emphasize his desire, "on the fraternization policy, you are my 'no compromise' point man for the effort. No compromise." He looked at me.

I nodded, "Understood, sir."

He leaned back again and raised a third finger, "The Quadrennial Defense Review (QDR) is your baby, and I'll let the rest of Marine Corps leadership know that they must support all of your efforts. We have a solid story to tell, so don't let the other services or anyone in the Department of Defense, beat you down."

His three main issues and challenges, coupled with ongoing readiness issues, occasional travel to visit with the Marines and sailors around the world, and Congressional testimony assured me of a very busy two years as the ACMC.

Immediately it was obvious we had our work cut out for us in terms of protecting our Bell Boeing V-22 Osprey program from the knives of the budget cutters. The thing that made the Osprey revolutionary was it combined the functionality of a conventional helicopter with the long range, high-speed cruise performance of a turbo-prop aircraft. Our plan was that, once operational, it would replace the medium-lift CH-46 Helicopter which was based on old technology and introduced to the Marine Corps back when I was in Vietnam.

BELL BOEING V-22 OSPREY

Because the Osprey was so revolutionary with its complex leap-ahead technology, it became a recurring topic in Congress with loud, vocal, competing factions that spoke for and against it. It was a favorite target of all the naysayers who argued that the technology just wasn't there—and, even if it was, the cost per aircraft would be prohibitive. Support for it within the Pentagon was minimal, and there were ongoing threats that the Secretary of Defense was going to kill the program. I can still recall a meeting where the comptroller for the DOD said, "We will give you as many Blackhawk helicopters as you want at no cost if you'll just drop the Osprey!"

"Well, that's obviously not my decision," I said. "I'll go back and present the offer to General Krulak, but my recommendation to him will be that we reject the offer. Trust me, we aren't going to fall off the development and fielding of this aircraft!"

Both General Krulak and I agreed that what the comptroller offered was unacceptable. The Blackhawk helicopter is a great helicopter, but it was a poor substitute as a replacement for our medium-lift helicopter requirement.

Thankfully, the program continued to be supported by Congress, who has always been our friend in Washington—our only friend, some would say. Time and time again, our leadership, from the commandant on down, would visit Capitol Hill and walk the halls of Congress, articulating the Osprey's advanced technology. Prudently, many of the various parts that went into the production of the Osprey were manufactured in various states around the country. The job potential in the various states represented by Congress was obvious to the members and, coupled with that members of Congress trusted the Marine Corps and its leadership, their continued support of the program was assured. [Interestingly, now that the V-22 has proven itself, all the services want them.]

Perhaps my most challenging responsibility during my tenure as ACMC was engaging in the development of the Quadrennial Defense Review (QDR), a legislatively mandated review of DOD strategy, programs, and resources. Within the context of DOD's strategy, priorities, and any perceived threats, this report was to be a very comprehensive look at force structure, modernization plans, and the budget to support them. The QDR was due to Congress every four years, and the first one was slated for completion in 1997. Each of the services, agencies, and departments that made up the DOD had to defend their budgets, their programs, and their end strengths.

Since it was the first time we were doing it, everyone took cautious steps, trying to protect their piece of the DOD pie—their equities, their end strength, their programs, etc. The pressure was always on in terms of what we were discussing and what decisions might result from the review.

Working on the QDR was a long, laborious, all-encompassing process which occupied nearly half of my two-year term. Because it was such a mammoth undertaking, we had to meet at least twice a week. I had to know every program we had and how it fit in the big picture that made up the Marine Corps, and so did the other services and agencies that made up the DOD. Any time we learned something new of value, it gave us all a better appreciation of what comprised the DOD. Sure, we were each looking out for our own equities, but there also had to be some give and take on both sides.

The art of negotiation was critically important. One of the takeaways from my involvement with the QDR was the importance of being able to articulate your position and what you bring to the table for a big organization. Make no mistake, I had a cadre of top notch staff officers working overtime, making me smart on 'all things Marine.'

I found it to be a worthwhile exercise because it made all of us take an honest look at ourselves and become aware of the others' programs, capabilities, and limitations. Listening to others defend their organizations was an educational exercise, and I gained a new level of respect and appreciation for DOD in its entirety.

The Marine Corps didn't lose anything in the process of the QDR. Given that we are such a small organization, we were a pretty cheap alternative when you looked at the strategy and associated requirements. The little Marine Corps was a bargain compared to the budgets of the Army, Navy, Air Force and the other agencies within DOD.

Congressional committees routinely requested General Krulak and me to appear to testify before them. We spent a lot of time on Capitol Hill defending our positions on various programs. The topic might be manpower, for example. It was feasible that the three-star in charge of Manpower might be the one doing the testifying but, most of the time, I ended up testifying before committees with my counterparts from other services (who were called vices, not assistant commandants). We would sit at a table in front of the committees, deliver our opening statements and then field questions from the members. Sometimes the questions pertained to only one service, and its representative would answer. However, on most occasions, each of us would be asked to respond to the same question—which could get dicey unless all the services were in agreement on the issue at hand. You can imagine the discomfort this could cause to the representative whose response was not in line with that of the others who were testifying. Likewise, the nature and tone of the questions would very much depend on who was doing the asking and what side of the aisle they were on.

Naturally, the Democrats would try to support the Clinton administration and their president. Of course, it's not like they were all perfectly in step like a bunch of lemmings. There were Democrats who weren't in support of the White House's position on various issues. Generally speaking, however, when a member asking the questions was a Democrat, they would go easy on us. They generally tried to support whatever direction or position the White House might be pursuing at the time.

The Republicans, meanwhile, would take every opportunity to ask the tough questions that oftentimes were counter to, and critical of, the administration's position. Despite the question or the questioner, it was my obligation to answer each and every question truthfully and to the best of my ability—even when doing so was less than enjoyable. If I didn't know the answer or needed to provide additional detail, I would 'take it' (the question) 'for the record' and my folks would develop the answer and provide it to the members for their consideration.

Amphibious shipping and manpower end strength were always hot topics during congressional testimony, and it wasn't unusual for us to be in conflict with the Administration's position on these.

Testifying was something that seemed to go on endlessly, but I enjoyed it despite the mammoth amount of preparation that was involved. In advance of each committee hearing, all of the young action officers would come into my office with stacks of books and we would review and discuss the various issues that might be raised.

As I said, these were the Clinton years and with this liberal administration, came social issues we were forced to look at with an eye toward changing long held positions. One such issue that had recently become policy in the military was *Don't Ask, Don't Tell.* This policy meant that the military was not to ask about the sexual orientation of a service member, and the service member was not to disclose this information. It wasn't a perfect solution, but it was a good first step, and it worked. Our concerns that it would affect the good order and discipline required in the military were unfounded, and the troops seemed to adapt more quickly than did their leadership who, in many respects, were wedded to old ideas. Change is never easy and the first reaction to change is often resistance. But I was tasked by the commandant with ensuring that the Corps made this policy work and it did.

Fraternization was another contentious issue in which I was heavily involved. Defined as seniors dating and having relationships with juniors or between officers and enlisted, this has historically been considered unacceptable. It violates the rank structure and, potentially, the established chain of command. It was an issue that seemed to emerge shortly after the implementation of the *Don't Ask, Don't Tell* policy. Here again, the Administration was attempting to change a policy established in the military as essential to good order and discipline.

Complicating the discussion was that each of the services approached it differently. With the Army, surprisingly, the most liberal in its interpretation of this policy and, not unexpectedly, my Marine Corps the most rigid. I say surprisingly when referring to the Army's position because one would expect them to be on a par with the Marines in terms of their approach toward fraternization; both organizations are sized, structured and equipped for the same type of mission. Discipline on the battlefield is such an imperative, it starts at boot camp and stays with you all the way until you end your service, whether that be three or 30 years later. We could well anticipate that, at any time, we might have to ask our Marines to put themselves in harm's way, and this solemn responsibility demanded absolute discipline unencumbered by any personal relationships that might exist as a result of a relaxation in the fraternization policy.

This issue was being hotly debated inside the Pentagon to the point that the Secretary of Defense instructed all of the services to develop and implement one policy on fraternization. Following up on this edict, the head DOD lawyer assembled all of the vices of the various services and me, and presented a lengthy briefing on what she believed the fraternization policy should be. Her position was most closely aligned with that held by the Army, inasmuch as she wanted to relax the strict interpretation of fraternization and adopt a more benign and less rigid approach.

My counterparts in the other services were reticent on the subject because they undoubtedly knew that I would not hesitate to push back on the brief and the policy—and how right they were. After the attorney's lengthy briefing she sat, leaning back in her chair. I was the first one to speak.

"That may be the way you think you're going to do things," I said, "but there is no way I am going to agree. Not in the least." The DOD counsel's posture stiffened at that; she now sat ramrod straight in her chair as I continued. "This—what you're proposing—isn't good in any way, shape or form and we aren't going to support it. It's important to remember the military is not a democracy; troops do not get to vote on what they can or cannot do." Her eyes narrowed and I sensed she was about to interrupt me. I held a hand up and she let me continue. "To allow that would erode the structure of the chain of command. Officer-enlisted relationships could and would lead to a toxic climate; seniors in relationships with juniors weakens discipline and could destroy unit integrity. And good order, discipline and the sanctity of the chain of command are the very bedrock of our Corps!" I was unequivocal when I said, "I cannot speak for my commandant, but I won't accept it and I know my commandant won't." I shook my head, watched the look on her face harden even further, and kept going, "Marines are formed, shaped and trained to be ready for combat; readiness is non-negotiable and anything that detracts from that absolute requirement—as what you're proposing would do—is not open to compromise or discussion."

A relaxation of the fraternization prohibition never came to pass. I am not sure the Marine Corps would have accepted fraternization even if it had been ordered.

One of the most important initiatives, among many, that General Krulak instituted was a change to the training conducted at our two recruit depots. He called me to his office to brief me on it:

"I really need your help on this one; I want to introduce a new challenge to boot camp, the Crucible." [He explained, at length, what he was proposing and that detail follows below this conversation.]

I told him, "Whoa! You know there'll be pushback from all quarters of the Marine Corps." I shook my head. "They'll say if it— boot camp—isn't broken... why fix it?"

"You're right, that's exactly what they'll say." He studied me for a moment and then continued. "I believe, that the Crucible will add the final element to making our Marines truly ready for combat." He grew silent—eyes locked on mine—and I knew he was gauging how I felt about what he was proposing. I could also tell how much he believed that this change would greatly benefit our Marines and the Corps.

"I'm with you on this; I see great similarities with it and with what I experienced and learned at Getlin's Corner. Those hours changed me forever." I looked down for a moment, considered what I had just said and realized how very true it was. I looked up and caught General Krulak's nod.

"I get what you mean, Butch, and agree. Seeing it firsthand... what it means in battle. That's what I want our Marines to understand and for them to get the sense of it during their training."

I returned his nod, my mind still on Hill 70, and continued, "Anything that prepares Marines, that makes them better, has all my support." I matched his look. "Times have changed and as always the Marine Corps should be out in front in adapting to change. Likewise, the young men and women coming into the Corps are different from in the past and we need to recognize that. Most are focused on themselves and not those on their right and left."

"You're spot on, Butch." General Krulak leaned forward and slapped his right hand on the desktop. "The challenge has changed and the kids are different. That's one of the reasons for the new recruiting messages we're putting out—to attract young people but do it in such a way that we also give them a certain expectation of what they can take away from the experience." He sat back and shook his head. "But an advertising message won't help them become better Marines—it won't improve on how we teach them that essential element, that core, of what it truly means to be a Marine."

"As I understand your intent," I felt the energy of what he was proposing and how much impact it would have on young men and women, "the Crucible is aimed to fix that. It makes the fire team and the squad, the Marines that make them up, invaluable to the success of the whole."

"That's it. Exactly." His eyes gleamed and I knew this could be one of the things he and I could both do that would have a permanent, constructive, effect on the Marine Corps.

"If we do this right," I told him, "the Marines will see this and embrace it. They'll see the strength of teamwork and the unit, as opposed to that of the individual, in accomplishing the task at hand or the assigned mission. They'll see the wisdom of looking out for each other and to do whatever is necessary to protect each other while accomplishing the mission. This is long overdue, sir. I'm convinced we can make this—the making of a Marine—the capstone event of boot camp. You can count on me not only as an advocate but also an apostle."

This—incorporating the Crucible into recruit training—was an unprecedented step. He knew full well that he was treading on thin ice by even suggesting a change in what was viewed by all as a solid, well established and proven training schedule for making Marines. He knew equally well that, in implementing this change, he was leaving himself open to criticism he was making change for change's sake. What he was adding to the already daunting training regime would take place at the end of boot camp, beginning during week eleven and overlapping into week twelve. The Crucible was developed to become a nonstop simulation of battlefield experience—a mini-war scenario. The Marine Corps website (Marines.com) describes it in this way:

> *The Crucible is the final phase of Marine Corps recruit training that tests every skill learned and every value instilled. Recruits will be challenged for 54 continuous hours with little food and sleep. To complete this final test, recruits must have the heart, the intestinal fortitude, the body, the mind, the desire and the ability. The recruits must pull together or fall apart. Win as one or all will fail. Succeed and you will carry a sense of accomplishment that will last forever.*

Recruits go through the Crucible as members of a squad, with those they have trained alongside for weeks. What the website says bears restating—and emphasizing: together, they do whatever is necessary to get their squad through this event, including carrying each other's packs, dragging each other along, and doing whatever they have to do to make sure that they all finish the Crucible together. Without a doubt, during the Crucible, they are telling themselves and their squad mates, *we can make it! We can do this! We've been in boot camp for eleven weeks, and we just have to get through the next 54 hours.* They have to use every resource available to them, both internal and external. This instills in them a don't-quit mentality and a code, to look out for their fellow Marines, that will last a lifetime. They enter into the culminating ceremony exhausted and dirty but incredibly proud as their drill instructor walks down the line and hands each of them their eagle, globe and anchor emblem. Their graduation from the Crucible is the first time they are called a Marine, and their rite of passage is complete.

As I mentioned earlier, the first reaction to change is always resistance. There were plenty of people from both the active duty community and the retired community who were against the idea, and it is a testament to General Krulak that he was willing to take the risk in the face of such resistance. I was his greatest supporter in this effort, as I saw it as the ideal means for avoiding future Getlin's Corners.

After all, here we were, introducing to our young Marines the fundamental—foundational—concept of Brotherhood and instilling in them the absolute commitment to look out for each other. Today's Marines agree that the Crucible is the premier event of boot camp, and I can't help but feel that somewhere, Jack Loweranitis and John Bobo, along with our other thirteen fallen Brothers, are smiling down in agreement every time a new team of recruits completes the Crucible.

* * *

Perhaps my very favorite part of being the Assistant Commandant was that I was able to get away from the Pentagon and travel around the entire Marine Corps to see the troops. That was when I was most in my element. Kathy often traveled with me and met with the wives and families of those we visited. We traveled to almost all of the bases and stations where Marines and their families were located, both in the States and overseas. It was terrific to get out, meet and talk with the young Marines and their families. It gave me an opportunity to see where they lived, worked and trained, and assess their readiness and the readiness of their equipment.

TALKING WITH A YOUNG CAPTAIN DURING AN EXERCISE AT CAMP LEJEUNE

I got to fly in every aircraft in the Marine inventory, to ride and drive every vehicle we had, and to shoot every weapons system (not always hitting the target, I might add.) I was able to practice eyeball level leadership at every stop and always came away reinvigorated by the experience. While on these trips, Kathy would meet with the families of the Marines, get to hear firsthand how things were going from their perspective, and share her observations with me. This was invaluable as it allowed me to take immediate action in the event something needed to be fixed, changed or modified. With a practiced and critical eye, she visited the hospitals, post exchanges, commissaries, schools and living quarters to ensure that they met the needs of the Marine families.

PREPARING FOR A ST. PATRICK'S DAY PARADE IN HOLYOKE, MASSACHUSETTS

A special and memorable occasion that took place on Memorial Day in 1997 occurred when I was invited to be the Grand Marshal for my hometown parade. Leading the parade through the town in my full-dress uniform, and seeing everyone I knew and loved, was fantastic and something I will never forget. I was seen as 'their general' and could not have been prouder of being a true Townie and Hullonian.

I was approached by many firemen and policemen who were taking part in the parade and wanted to meet and talk to me. They all knew me from Desert Storm and the news releases that would come out in the local paper each time I received a promotion. Many of these folks were the sons of guys I grew up with in Hull. The town was so small, we all knew each other in one way or another, and everyone knew that I was the hometown boy, who became a Marine and a four-star general.

Another highlight of my tenure as ACMC was my visit to the White House and meeting with President Clinton. [I had been to the White House before but this visit was particularly memorable.] Kathy and I attended a Memorial Day breakfast at the White House in 1998 along with about a hundred other folks representing the various military organizations in the country. After the breakfast, we all got in line to shake hands with President Clinton and have our picture taken with him.

Well, it just so happened that the week preceding that breakfast, both the president and I had been up in Springfield, Massachusetts on separate occasions giving speeches. So, when it was our turn to meet him, I said, "Good to meet you, Mr. President, and by the way, I was in Springfield giving a speech last week and everyone was still talking about your recent visit up there!" Before I brought up his speech, he seemed like a paper cut out, perfunctorily shaking hands with everyone and thanking them for coming. Now, it was as if a switch had been flipped inside of him. He suddenly became very animated and excited. "Great, General!" he said. "It was a terrific trip, and I really enjoyed it." He went on and on for a minute or two that was so surreal it seemed to last an hour. The Secret Service and protocol folks were anxious to keep the line moving, so they worked overtime to end the conversation.

From there, we all traveled to Arlington National Cemetery where President Clinton laid a wreath at the Tomb of the Unknown Soldier and delivered his speech. As he was exiting with the Secret Service, he caught sight of me out of the corner of his eye and busted through the crowd so he could come over to me. "General Neal, I'm so glad you told me about that Springfield thing!" And then we started chatting again.

It was easy to understand President Clinton's tremendous success as a politician. Despite all the things he had on his mind that day, and the fact that he'd just given a speech and was tired, he went out of his way to come over and tell me how happy he was that I had brought up his speech in Springfield. He was used to remembering faces, remembering names, remembering events. Even more importantly, his enthusiasm was almost contagious. He was bursting with energy and excitement to get hold of me again just so he could say to me in so many words, "That was indeed a great event in Springfield, and I am thankful to you for reminding me of it and bringing it to my attention!" Sometimes we think of politicians as subhuman or above the fray, but in that exchange with me, he demonstrated and showed the importance of remembering events and the personalities associated with them.

CHAPTER 32

RETIREMENT: MOVING ON

"Choose a job you love, and you will never have to work a day in your life." --Confucius

My two years as Assistant Commandant of the Marine Corps flew by. The events, issues and responsibilities I have described ensured that I was busy from the day I became ACMC until the day I stepped down. General Krulak and I were a good team, and I was always comfortable in my role as his ACMC and happy working with and for him. In selecting me, the general had gone in a different direction than anticipated, that's for sure. I think he caught a lot of people by surprise with his selection, including me. Fortunately, it seemed to work out well for all parties—the commandant, the Corps and me.

I had become assistant commandant in 1996 when I was 54 years old, and having reached the end of my tenure two years later in 1998, there was nowhere else to go in the Marine Corps. I had moved up through the ranks more quickly than most. I was only a general officer for a little over seven years, having been promoted to one-star general in 1990 and retiring as a four-star in 1998.

Retirement was not something I had spent much time considering and now, suddenly, the time had come. Truthfully, I would have loved to stay in uniform if another four-star opportunity had been available to me at the time, but such was not the case. In retrospect, I must say that 54 or 55 is not a bad age to retire. At that age, I was still a viable asset if I wanted to go out into the civilian world and continue my professional life, whether that meant starting a new career or serving as a director on various boards.

The die was cast and, on August 26th, 1998, I retired from the Marine Corps. My retirement ceremony was held literally in my backyard at the Marine Barracks at 8th and I Streets. The event took place around seven o'clock on an evening made very hot and humid by an approaching hurricane that was moving up the coast from the south.

My family was there, along with those who knew me from my hometown of Hull. There were some of my surviving Brothers from India 3/9 and people from other services I had come to know over the years. I invited friends from my nearly 35 years in the Marine Corps, both active duty and retired, as well those Kathy and I had known socially from all of our assignments. Looking out at the sea of faces, I saw a panoply of folks who had contributed to any success I had enjoyed as a Marine or impacted my life in some way.

There was a terrific group of folks there from South Boston led by Tommy Lyons, a Marine Vietnam veteran who was and is the 'go to guy' for any issues in Massachusetts dealing with veterans. A funny but typical incident with this contingent occurred the day of my ceremony. Fearing that we might run out of beer at the retirement party following the ceremony, they arrived early at the entrance to the Barracks with quite a few cases of beer for the festivities. At first the Marines on duty were reluctant to let them in, but somehow the Southie Marines prevailed and I am happy to report we indeed did not run out of beer!

Prior to moving out to the parade deck, General Krulak and his wife Zandi invited our whole family to the Home of the Commandant for a private social and for picture-taking, which was special for Kathy and our three children.

SIGNING THE GUEST LOG AT THE HOME OF THE COMMANDANT WITH MY FAMILY PRIOR TO MY RETIREMENT CEREMONY

The ceremony itself was wonderful. General Krulak was the host, and the sequence of events followed along traditional lines and included a parade. Of course, this was extra special for me, as it was in my honor. There were two companies of Marines in blues and whites in front, marching on, along with the Drum and Bugle Corps, and I could not have imagined a more perfect way to end my career.

I stood out there alone at the position of attention; dressed in my Blue/White 'B' uniform with medals adorning my chest and four stars on each shoulder. The American flag waved behind me as they called everyone to attention. Then they read the retirement documents and a letter from President Clinton thanking me for my service, as well as letters from the Secretary of Defense, Secretary of the Navy and Chairman of the Joint Chiefs of Staff. Then they presented me with the Defense Distinguished Service Medal. After the announcer, had read the award citation and the retirement documents they brought out Kathy and presented her with an award for her significant contributions over the years to all Marines and sailors and their families.

These awards presentations were followed by remarks from General Krulak, who was emotional in his comments about me and about the team that he and I had become over our two action-packed years. He emphasized my moral courage in the fraternization debates and my unyielding commitment to addressing the issues raised during the Quadrennial Defense Review deliberations. He spoke of my loyalty to him and to our Corps and closed by saying, "As a result of General Neal's efforts, the Marine Corps is much better off today than it was two years ago," he gestured for me to come forward and speak.

RECEIVING MY RETIREMENT CERTIFICATE FROM GENERAL KRULAK

I focused on what I had experienced over my years in the Marine Corps, and on having enjoyed the enviable opportunity to work with, and learn from, some of the finest men and women our country has to offer. I acknowledged the presence of many of those who had a special place in my journey, from those in my hometown to my Brothers from Getlin's Corner to those in my various commands, to those special leaders who mentored me along the way.

There was Ernie Minelli, who had given me my job on the rubbish truck and kept me employed for six years so that I could attend college.

Looking at the face of my Brother from India 3/9, John Prickett, I was reminded of that long-ago battle that served as the defining moment in my life and became the catalyst for my decision to stay in the Marine Corps.

I spoke about John Bobo and my fifteen Brothers who perished on that terrible and tragic night of March 30–31st, 1967, and how I carried their memory within me. "It is my solemn obligation to remember my fallen Brothers and I will remember them all until the day I die. And though I am now taking off my uniform, I will die a Marine and be buried a Marine."

I concluded by thanking my wife Kathy and my son Andrew and two daughters, Amy and Erin, for their love and unfailing support throughout the years. Then I shared my favorite quote from President John F. Kennedy:

> "For of those to whom much is given, much is required {and expected}. And when at some future date the high court of history sits in judgment on each of us, recording whether in our brief span of service we fulfilled our responsibilities to the state, our success or failure, in whatever office we hold, will be measured by the answer to four questions: First, were we truly men and women of courage.... Second, were we truly men and women of judgment.... Third, were we truly men and women of integrity.... Finally, were we truly men and women of dedication?"

I felt confident that I could answer, "Yes," to each of those questions. My remarks were followed by honors as they fired a seventeen-gun salute. Then, with Kathy at my side, the band and Marines marched by in a Pass in Review. My emotions were in turmoil as I accepted the fact that it was my last day in uniform. And reminded myself, it was not my last day as a Marine. I would be a proud United States Marine until my last breath.

"When good men die,
their goodness does not perish."
~ *Euripides*

Afterword

"All I am and all I have is at the service of my country."

--General Stonewall Jackson

2016

My wife and I live on Capitol Hill, about two miles from the Lincoln Memorial. To the right of the Lincoln Memorial is the Vietnam Wall, which reportedly receives a greater number of annual visitors than any other site in Washington, D.C. Whenever I am asked why the Vietnam Wall is such a magnet for visitors, I say that it's the names that make this monument so compelling. Each name represents a real person, someone who gave his or her all for their comrades in a distant country in an unpopular war.

On the Folger Shakespeare Theater, there is a quote by writer/poet Ben Jonson, and I see it every day when I walk my dog: "Thou art a monument without a tomb and art alive still while thy book doth live and we have wits to read and praise to give..." I believe this quote applies not only to Shakespeare's works but by substituting a few words in the quote it has great relevance to the Wall and the names inscribed on it: "Thou art a monument without a tomb and art alive still while the Wall doth stand and we have wits to read the names and honor to give..."

For years, I avoided visiting the Wall for reasons I cannot articulate, even to myself. Now I can't seem to stay away. It is a solemn place and the quiet demeanor of those visiting the Wall is comforting and always appreciated. It is obvious that those walking beside the black granite panels feel a sense of wonder and reverence for those whose names are chiseled on its Spartan surface.

Now, as I make my way down the Wall, I arrive at panel 17-E, Row 70, a place I know quite well. At eye level, the first familiar name to catch my eye is that of John P. Bobo, a Marine lieutenant. In a cluster surrounding his name are the names of those fourteen other Marines from Company I, 3rd Battalion, 9th Marine Regiment, 3rd Marine Division (India Company 3/9) who died on the night of March 30—31st, 1967. Rank and organization are not listed on the Wall, only names, but we surviving Brothers from India 3/9 know these names as we know no others. They are Pfc. Albert G. Antler, Pfc. Rubin M. Armenta, Cpl. James E. Blevins, Pfc. Edward E. Cannon, Lance Cpl. Larry H. Crumbaker, Capt. Michael P. Getlin, Pfc. Donald W. Krick, Cpl. John L. Loweranitis, Cpl. Walter J. Nerad, Jr., Capt. Ralph B. Pappas, Cpl. David A. Siemon, Pfc. Frank H. Thomas, Jr., Pfc. Wallace Williams, and Lance Cpl. Roman R. Villamor, Jr.

I usually spend a few minutes looking at that panel. As I stand there, the first thing that goes through my mind is the randomness of war; why some die and others survive. I think of the lost potential represented on the Wall, all 58,315 who died in the Vietnam War and whose names are etched on that black granite. Of course, I am especially moved by the names of my fifteen Brothers; I did not know all of them personally but the sense of comradeship and the dangers we shared ensured that they would always remain in my memory and be a part of my life. I continue my walk, deep in reflection as I head back down the Wall and up toward my home.

All the men in India 3/9 were family. When we use the term 'Brothers,' we don't use it loosely. And there is nothing like the cauldron of combat to intensify that brotherhood even further.

As it states on the Marine Corps website:

"*Semper Fidelis* distinguishes the Marine Corps bond from any other. It goes beyond teamwork—it is a brotherhood that can always be counted on. Latin for "always faithful," *Semper Fidelis* became the Marine Corps motto in 1883. It guides Marines to be faithful to the mission at hand, to each other, to the Corps and to country, no matter what. Becoming a Marine is a transformation that cannot be undone, and *Semper Fidelis* is a permanent reminder of that. Once made, a Marine will forever live by the ethics and values of the Corps."

From a geographical standpoint, I live closer to the Wall than any of the other survivors from India Company 3/9. In some way, I feel like I'm their representative.

The walks I take to the Wall help keep alive the memories of those we lost. I once read in a book about Vietnam that those who survived have a solemn responsibility to remember and keep alive the memory of those who died. I agree. This obligation is probably why I ultimately decided to stay in the Marine Corps, not only to not forget those who died but just as importantly to do my damnedest to try to ensure that future Marines do not have to experience a Getlin's Corner because of poor leadership.

POST SCRIPT

Recently, as was my custom, I stopped at the Vietnam Wall just to see the names and think for a few minutes about my Brothers.

As I stood in front of Panel 17E looking at the fifteen names all clustered around row 70, a little elderly lady (a grandmother type, my age) moved almost in front of me.

I was about to step back to give her more room when I realized she was one of the volunteers that help people at the Wall find names, and learn the history, etc. She was polite and said she was looking for row 70. I pointed it out to her and asked. "What name are you looking for?"

VIEW OF THE WASHINGTON MONUMENT FROM PANEL 17-E OF THE VIETNAM WALL

"John Bobo." Her eyes hadn't stopped scanning the names.

I almost fell over. I pointed to his name.

"Thank you. I'm doing a pencil etching of his name. Someone requested it on our web site," she said.

Talk about coincidence, it's a small world, whatever, but it was an amazing happenstance. "John was a Medal of Honor recipient," I told her. She immediately checked her list, nodding her head when she saw that was so. "Thank you for what you're doing," I told her then turned away to continue my walk, happy in spite of the fact that it was cold, raining and the cherry blossoms had not yet exploded. There were those—other than me—who would not let my Brothers be forgotten.

What happened that morning leads me to close with this as it ties back to that most significant moment in my life. There is a story, perhaps apocryphal, that in late 1968, during a Viet Cong mortar attack against Tan Son Nhut Air Base in Saigon, a memorial chapel was destroyed. A few days later as a chaplain passed by its ruins, his eye caught the glimmer of an object among the rubble. It was a board upon which was inscribed a poem of unknown origin:

> *Not for fame or reward,*
> *Not for place or rank,*
> *Not lured by ambition*
> *or goaded by necessity,*
> *But in simple obedience*
> *as they understood it.*
> *These men suffered all,*
> *dared all, and died.*
> *Lest we forget...lest we forget...*

--Butch Neal, 2017
Washington, D.C.

ABOUT THE AUTHOR

General Richard 'Butch' Neal is a retired four-star general and served from 1996—1998 as Assistant Commandant of the U. S. Marine Corps. He was born in the small town of Hull, Massachusetts, and went on to carry those solid small town values with him into a long and distinguished career in the Marine Corps, the smallest of the major military services.

After graduating with a B.S. in History and Education from Northeastern University in Boston, Neal was commissioned as a second lieutenant and spent the next 35 years commanding at every level. During his time in the Marine Corps, he also went on to graduate from the National War College and earn his M.Ed. from Tulane University in New Orleans.

The author served two tours in the Republic of Vietnam, and during Desert Storm, served as the Deputy Director of Operations for General Schwarzkopf as well as Central Command Briefer. As a result of the many televised international press briefings he delivered during the war, General Neal returned home to discover that he'd become a household name and a nationally recognized figure.

General Neal's decorations include the Defense Distinguished Service Medal; Silver Star Medal with Gold Star; the Defense Superior Service Medal with Palm; Bronze Star Medal with Combat V; and the Purple Heart.

Since retiring in 1998, General Neal has been president of three intellectual property companies. He was the Senior Mentor for the United States Marine Corps for five years and is currently a

Senior Fellow at the National Defense University. The general also served as Chairman of the Board for the Military Officers Association of America, is presently on the board of directors for several companies, and sits on the Board of Trustees for Norwich University.

First and foremost, Butch Neal is a family man. He is the proud father of three children, Andrew, Amy, and Erin, and cherishes his role as Grampa Guy to Marina, Nathaniel, Aiden, Kennedy, Tegan, Dominic, Sophia and Holland. He also maintains relationships with many of his Brothers in his Marine Corps family.

When he is not spending time on Capitol Hill with Kathy, his wife of 48 years, and their kids and grandkids, or visiting his hometown of Hull, he can often be found reading or running. And he can frequently be seen walking along the Vietnam Wall near his home, honoring and remembering his fifteen Brothers from India Company 3/9 who died on March 30—31st, 1967 at the Battle of Getlin's Corner. He considers it his solemn duty to remember his fallen Brothers, and believes that, in the remembering of them, they live on.

CPSIA information can be obtained
at www.ICGtesting.com
Printed in the USA
FSHW010346051019
62635FS